DATE DUE

MY 2 1 7	MY 1 7 '00		
AP 28 '98	MAR 19 2004		
MY 12 '98			
RENEW			
JY 11 '96			
AP 20			
AP 0 1 '00			

Modern Critical Interpretations

Charles Dickens's
Hard Times

Modern Critical Interpretations

These and other titles in preparation

Charles Dickens's
Hard Times

Edited and with an introduction by

Harold Bloom
Sterling Professor of the Humanities
Yale University

Chelsea House Publishers ◊ *1987*

NEW YORK ◊ NEW HAVEN ◊ PHILADELPHIA

©1987 by Chelsea House Publishers, a division
of Chelsea House Educational Communications, Inc.,
   95 Madison Avenue, New York, NY 10016
   345 Whitney Avenue, New Haven, CT 06511
   5014 West Chester Pike, Edgemont, PA 19028

Introduction ©1987 by Harold Bloom

Printed and bound in the United States of America

∞ The paper used in this publication meets the minimum
requirements of the American National Standard for Permanence of Paper for Printed Library Materials,
Z39.48–1984.

Library of Congress Cataloging-in-Publication Data
Charles Dickens's Hard times.
   (Modern critical interpretations)
   Bibliography: p.
   Includes index.
   Summary: A collection of eight critical essays on the
Dickens novel, arranged in chronological order of original
publication.
   1. Dickens, Charles, 1812–1870.   Hard times.
   [1. Dickens, Charles, 1812–1870.   Hard times.
   2. English literature — History and criticism]
   I. Bloom, Harold.   II. Series.
PR4561.C46   1987   823'.8   87–5186
ISBN 0-87754-737-8 (alk. paper)

Contents

Editor's Note

This book gathers together a representative selection of what I judge to be the best criticism of Charles Dickens's novel *Hard Times.* The critical essays are reprinted here in the chronological order of their original publication. I am grateful to Susan Laity, Henry Finder, and Shawn Rosenheim for their aid in editing this volume.

My introduction first considers Dickens's rhetorical stance as an instance of what John Ruskin called "stage fire" and then applies this critical trope to the appreciation of *Hard Times.* The renowned British Marxist critic Raymond Williams begins the chronological sequence of criticism with a brief reflection upon Dickens's hatred of Utilitarianism. Robert E. Lougy centers upon genre, reading *Hard Times* as a Radical version of romance.

An overview of the relationship between imagery and theme in *Hard Times* by Robert Barnard is followed by Geoffrey Thurley's consideration of caricature and character in the novel. Joseph Butwin contributes an account of the first appearance of the book in *Household Words,* and of the impressions that such a context would have been likely to foster.

An analysis of broken communication in *Hard Times* by Peter Bracher is complemented here by Roger Fowler's semiotic investigation of the novel. Steven Connor concludes this book with a deconstruction of *Hard Times,* showing us clearly the specifics of this narrative's "critical difference from itself."

Introduction

Courage would be the critical virtue most required if anyone were to attempt an essay that might be called "The Limitations of Shakespeare." Tolstoy, in his most outrageous critical performance, more or less tried just that, with dismal results, and even Ben Jonson might not have done much better had he sought to extend his ambivalent *obiter dicta* on his great friend and rival. Nearly as much courage, or foolhardiness, is involved in discoursing on the limitations of Dickens, but the young Henry James had a critical gusto that could carry him through every literary challenge. Reviewing *Our Mutual Friend* in 1865, James exuberantly proclaimed that "*Bleak House* was forced; *Little Dorrit* was labored; the present work is dug out as with a spade and pickaxe." At about this time, reviewing *Drum-Taps,* James memorably dismissed Whitman as an essentially prosaic mind seeking to lift itself, by muscular exertion, into poetry. To reject some of the major works of the strongest English novelist and the greatest American poet, at about the same moment, is to set standards for critical audacity that no one since has been able to match, even as no novelist since has equalled Dickens, nor any poet, Walt Whitman.

James was at his rare worst in summing up Dickens's supposedly principal inadequacy:

> Such scenes as this are useful in fixing the limits of Mr. Dickens's insight. Insight is, perhaps, too strong a word; for we are convinced that it is one of the chief conditions of his genius not to see beneath the surface of things. If we might hazard a definition of his literary character, we should, accordingly, call him the greatest of superficial novelists. We are aware that this

1

definition confines him to an inferior rank in the department of letters which he adorns; but we accept this consequence of our proposition. It were, in our opinion, an offence against humanity to place Mr. Dickens among the greatest novelists. For, to repeat what we have already intimated, he has created nothing but figure. He has added nothing to our understanding of human character. He is master of but two alternatives: he reconciles us to what is commonplace, and he reconciles us to what is odd. The value of the former service is questionable; and the manner in which Mr. Dickens performs it sometimes conveys a certain impression of charlatanism. The value of the latter service is incontestable, and here Mr. Dickens is an honest, an admirable artist.

This can be taken literally, and then transvalued: to see truly the surface of things, to reconcile us at once to the commonplace and the odd — these are not minor gifts. In 1860, John Ruskin, the great seer of the surface of things, the charismatic illuminator of the commonplace and the odd together, had reached a rather different conclusion from that of the young Henry James five years before James's brash rejection:

The essential value and truth of Dickens's writings have been unwisely lost sight of by many thoughtful persons merely because he presents his truth with some colour of caricature. Unwisely, because Dickens's caricature, though often gross, is never mistaken. Allowing for his manner of telling them, the things he tells us are always true. I wish that he could think it right to limit his brilliant exaggeration to works written only for public amusement; and when he takes up a subject of high national importance, such as that which he handled in *Hard Times,* that he would use severer and more accurate analysis. The usefulness of that work (to my mind, in several respects, the greatest he has written) is with many persons seriously diminished because Mr. Bounderby is a dramatic monster, instead of a characteristic example of a worldly master; and Stephen Blackpool a dramatic perfection, instead of a characteristic example of an honest workman. But let us not lose the use of Dickens's wit and insight, because he chooses to speak in a circle of stage fire. He is entirely right in his main drift and purpose in every book he has written; and all of them, but especially *Hard Times,* should be studied with close and earnest care by persons interested in social questions. They will find much that is partial, and, because partial, apparently unjust; but if they examine all the evidence on the other side, which Dickens seems to overlook, it will appear, after all their trouble, that his view was the finally right one, grossly and sharply told.

To say of Dickens that he chose "to speak in a circle of stage fire" is exactly right, since Dickens is the greatest actor among novelists, the finest master of dramatic projection. A superb stage performer, he never stops performing in his novels, which is not the least of his many Shakespearean characteristics. Martin Price usefully defines some of these as "his effortless invention, his brilliant play of language, the scope and density of his imagined world." I like also Price's general comparison of Dickens to the strongest satirist in the language, Swift, a comparison that Price shrewdly turns into a confrontation:

But the confrontation helps us to define differences as well: Dickens is more explicit, more overtly compassionate, insisting always upon the perversions of feeling as well as of thought. His outrage is of the same consistency as his generous celebration, the satirical wit of the same copious extravagance as the comic elaborations. Dickens' world is alive with things that snatch, lurch, teeter, thrust, leer; it is the animate world of Netherlandish genre painting or of Hogarth's prints, where all space is a field of force, where objects vie or intrigue with each other, where every human event spills over into the things that surround it. This may become the typically crowded scene of satire, where persons are reduced to things and things to matter in motion; or it may pulsate with fierce energy and noisy feeling. It is different from Swift; it is the distinctive Dickensian plenitude, which we find again in his verbal play, in his great array of vivid characters, in his massed scenes of feasts or public declamations. It creates rituals as compelling as the resuscitation of Rogue Riderhood, where strangers participate solemnly in the recovery of a spark of life, oblivious for the moment of the unlovely human form it will soon inhabit.

That animate, Hogarthian world, "where all space is a field of force," indeed is a plenitude and it strikes me that Price's vivid description suggests Rabelais rather than Swift as a true analogue. Dickens, like Shakespeare in one of many aspects and like Rabelais, is as much carnival as stage fire, a kind of endless festival. The reader of Dickens stands in the midst of a festival, which is too varied, too multiform, to be taken in even by innumerable readings. Something always escapes our ken; Ben Jonson's sense of being "rammed with life" is exemplified more even by Dickens than by Rabelais, in that near-Shakespearean plenitude that is Dickens's peculiar glory.

Is it possible to define that plenitude narrowly enough so as to conceptualize it for critical use, though by "conceptualize" one meant only a critical metaphor? Shakespearean representation is no touchstone for Dickens or for anyone else, since above all modes of representation it turns upon an inward changing brought about by characters listening to themselves speak. Dickens cannot do that. His villains are gorgeous, but there are no Iagos or Edmunds among them. The severer, more relevant test, which Dickens must fail, though hardly to his detriment, is Falstaff, who generates not only his own meaning, but meaning in so many others besides, both on and off the page. Probably the severest test is Shylock, most Dickensian of Shakespeare's characters, since we cannot say of Dickens's Shylock, Fagin, that there is much Shakespearean about him at all. Fagin is a wonderful grotesque, but the winds of will are not stirred in him, while they burn on hellishly forever in Shylock.

Carlyle's injunction, to work in the will, seems to have little enough place in the cosmos of the Dickens characters. I do not say this to indicate a limitation, or even a limit, nor do I believe that the will to live or the will to power is ever relaxed in or by Dickens. But nothing is got for nothing, except perhaps in or by Shakespeare, and Dickens purchases his kind of plenitude at the expense of one aspect of the will. T. S. Eliot remarked that "Dickens's characters are real because there is no one like them." I would modify that to "They are real because they are not like one another, though sometimes they are a touch more like some of us than like each other." Perhaps the will, in whatever aspect, can differ only in degree rather than in kind among us. The aesthetic secret of Dickens appears to be that his villains, heroes, heroines, victims, eccentrics, ornamental beings, do differ from one another *in the kinds of will that they possess*. Since that is hardly possible for us, as humans, it does bring about an absence in reality in and for Dickens. That is a high price to pay, but it is a good deal less than everything and Dickens got more than he paid for. We also receive a great deal more than we ever are asked to surrender when we read Dickens. That may indeed be his most Shakespearean quality, and may provide the critical trope I quest for in him. James and Proust hurt you more than Dickens does, and the hurt is the meaning, or much of it. What hurts in Dickens never has much to do with meaning, because there cannot be a poetics of pain where the will has ceased to be common or sadly uniform. Dickens really does offer a poetics of pleasure, which is surely worth our secondary uneasiness at his refusal to offer us any accurately mimetic representations of the human will. He writes always the book of the drives, which is why supposedly Freudian readings of him always fail so tediously. The conceptual metaphor he suggests in his representations of character and personality is neither Shakespearean mirror nor Romantic lamp, neither Rabelaisian carnival nor Fieldingesque open country. "Stage fire" seems to me perfect, for "stage" removes something of the reality of the will, yet only as modifier. The substantive remains "fire." Dickens is the poet of the fire of the drives, the true celebrant of Freud's myth of frontier concepts, of that domain lying on the border between psyche and body, falling into matter, yet partaking of the reality of both.

II

Hard Times is, for Dickens, a strikingly condensed novel, being about one-third of the length of *David Copperfield* and *Bleak House,* the two masterpieces that directly preceded it. Astonishing and aesthetically satisfying as it is, I believe it to be somewhat overpraised by modern criticism, or perhaps praised for some less than fully relevant reasons. Ruskin and Bernard Shaw after him admired the book as a testament to Dickens's conversion away from a commercialized and industrialized England and back towards a supposed juster and more humane society. But to like *Hard Times* because of its anti-Utilitarian ideology is to confuse the book with Carlyle and William Morris, as well as with Ruskin and Shaw. The most balanced judgment of the novel is that of Monroe Engel, who observes that "the greatest virtues of *Hard Times* are Dickens's characteristic virtues, but less richly present in the book than in many others." Gradgrind is poor stuff, and is not even an effective parody of Jeremy Bentham. The strength of the novel is indeed elsewhere, as we might expect in the theatrical Dickens.

And yet *Hard Times* is lacking in stage fire; compared to *Bleak House,* it possesses only a tiny component of the Sublime. Again, as an instance of the plain style, the mode of Esther Summerson's narrative, it is curiously weak, and has moreover such drab characterizations as Sissy Jupe and Stephen Blackpool. Indeed, the book's rhetoric is the most colorless in all of Dickens's work. Though, as Engel insisted, many of Dickens's authorial virtues are present, the book lacks the preternatural exuberance that makes Dickens unique among all novelists. Has it any qualities of its own to recommend our devotion?

I would suggest that the start of any critical wisdom about *Hard Times* is to dismiss every Marxist or other moral interpretation of the book. Yes, Dickens's heart was accurate, even if his notion of Benthamite social philosophy was not, and a great novelist's overt defense of imagination cannot fail to move us. Consider however the outrageous first chapter of *Hard Times,* "The One Thing Needful":

"Now, what I want is, Facts. Teach these boys and girls nothing but Facts. Facts alone are wanted in life. Plant nothing else, and root out everything else. You can only form the minds of reasoning animals upon Facts; nothing else will ever be of any service to them. This is the principle on which I bring up my own children, and this is the principle on which I bring up these children. Stick to Facts, sir!"

The scene was a plain, bare, monotonous vault of a schoolroom, and the speaker's square forefinger emphasized his observations by underscoring every sentence with a line on the schoolmaster's sleeve. The emphasis was helped by the speaker's square wall of a forehead, which had his eyebrows for its base, while his eyes found commodious cellarage in two dark caves, overshadowed by the wall. The emphasis was helped by the speaker's mouth, which was wide, thin, and hard set. The emphasis was helped by the speaker's voice, which was inflexible, dry, and dictatorial. The emphasis was helped by the speaker's hair, which bristled on the skirts of his bald head, a plantation of firs to keep the wind from its shining surface, all covered with knobs, like the crust of a plum pie, as if the head had scarcely warehouse-room for the hard facts stored inside. The speaker's obstinate carriage, square coat, square legs, square shoulders—nay, his very neckcloth, trained to take him by the throat with an unaccommodating grasp, like a stubborn fact, as it was—all helped the emphasis.

"In this life, we want nothing but Facts, sir; nothing but Facts!"

The speaker, and the schoolmaster, and the third grown

person present, all backed a little, and swept with their eyes
the inclined plane of little vessels then and there arranged in
order, ready to have imperial gallons of facts poured into
them until they were full to the brim.

Gradgrind is doubtless Dickens's ultimate revenge upon his own
school sufferings; Gradgrind might be called Murdstone run wild, except that Murdstone stays within the circle of caricature, whereas
Gradgrind's will is mad, is a drive towards death. And that is where, I
now think, the peculiar aesthetic strength of *Hard Times* is to be located.
The novel survives as phantasmagoria or nightmare, and hardly as a
societal or conceptual bad dream. What goes wrong in it is what Freud
called "family romances," which become family horrors. Critics always
have noted how really dreadful family relations are in *Hard Times,* as
they so frequently are elsewhere in Dickens. A particular power is
manifest if we analyze a passage near the conclusion of the penultimate
chapter of the first book of the novel, chapter 15, "Father and Daughter":

"Louisa," returned her father, "it appears to me that nothing
can be plainer. Confining yourself rigidly to Fact, the question
of Fact you state to yourself is: Does Mr. Bounderby ask me to
marry him? Yes, he does. The sole remaining question then is:
Shall I marry him? I think nothing can be plainer than that?"
"Shall I marry him?" repeated Louisa, with great deliberation.
"Precisely. And it is satisfactory to me, as your father, my
dear Louisa, to know that you do not come to the consideration of that question with the previous habits of mind, and
habits of life, that belong to many young women."
"No, father," she returned, "I do not."
"I now leave you to judge for yourself," said Mr. Gradgrind. "I have stated the case, as such cases are usually stated
among practical minds; I have stated it, as the case of your
mother and myself was stated in its time. The rest, my dear
Louisa, is for you to decide."
From the beginning, she had sat looking at him fixedly. As
he now leaned back in his chair, and bent his deep-set eyes
upon her in his turn, perhaps he might have seen one waver-
ing moment in her, when she was impelled to throw herself
upon his breast, and give him the pent-up confidences of her

heart. But, to see it, he must have overleaped at a bound the artificial barriers he had for many years been erecting, between himself and all those subtle essences of humanity which will elude the utmost cunning of algebra until the last trumpet ever to be sounded shall blow even algebra to wreck. The barriers were too many and too high for such a leap. With his unbending, utilitarian, matter-of-fact face, he hardened her again; and the moment shot away into the plumbless depths of the past, to mingle with all the lost opportunities that are drowned there.

Removing her eyes from him, she sat so long looking silently towards the town, that he said, at length: "Are you consulting the chimneys of the Coketown works, Louisa?"

"There seems to be nothing there but languid and monotonous smoke. Yet when the night comes, Fire bursts out, father!" she answered, turning quickly.

"Of course I know that, Louisa. I do not see the application of the remark." To do him justice he did not, at all.

She passed it away with a slight motion of her hand, and concentrating her attention upon him again, said, "Father, I have often thought that life is very short."—This was so distinctly one of his subjects that he interposed.

"It is short, no doubt, my dear. Still, the average duration of human life is proved to have increased of late years. The calculations of various life assurance and annuity offices, among other figures which cannot go wrong, have established the fact."

"I speak of my own life, father."

"O indeed? Still," said Mr. Gradgrind, "I need not point out to you, Louisa, that it is governed by the laws which govern lives in the aggregate."

"While it lasts, I would wish to do the little I can, and the little I am fit for. What does it matter?"

Mr. Gradgrind seemed rather at a loss to understand the last four words; replying, "How, matter? What matter, my dear?"

"Mr. Bounderby," she went on in a steady, straight way, without regarding this, "asks me to marry him. The question I have to ask myself is, shall I marry him? That is so, father, is it not? You have told me so, father. Have you not?"

"Certainly, my dear."

"Let it be so. Since Mr. Bounderby likes to take me thus, I am satisfied to accept his proposal. Tell him, father, as soon as you please, that this was my answer. Repeat it, word for word, if you can, because I should wish him to know what I said."

"It is quite right, my dear," retorted her father approvingly, "to be exact. I will observe your very proper request. Have you any wish in reference to the period of your marriage, my child?"

"None, father. What does it matter?"

Mr. Gradgrind had drawn his chair a little nearer to her, and taken her hand. But, her repetition of these words seemed to strike with some little discord on his ear. He paused to look at her, and, still holding her hand, said:

"Louisa, I have not considered it essential to ask you one question, because the possibility implied in it appeared to me to be too remote. But perhaps I ought to do so. You have never entertained in secret any other proposal?"

"Father," she returned, almost scornfully, "what other proposal can have been made to *me?* Whom have I seen? Where have I been? What are my heart's experiences?"

"My dear Louisa," returned Mr. Gradgrind, reassured and satisfied. "You correct me justly. I merely wished to discharge my duty."

"What do *I* know, father," said Louisa in her quiet manner, "of tastes and fancies; of aspirations and affections; of all that part of my nature in which such light things might have been nourished? What escape have I had from problems that could be demonstrated, and realities that could be grasped?" As she said it, she unconsciously closed her hand, as if upon a solid object, and slowly opened it as though she were releasing dust or ash.

Caricature here has leaped into Ruskin's "stage fire." Gradgrind, quite mad, nevertheless achieves the wit of asking Louisa whether she is consulting the oracular vapors of the Coketown chimneys. Her magnificent, "Yet when the night comes, Fire bursts out, father!" is more than a prophecy of the return of the repressed. It prophesies also the exuberance of Dickens himself, which comes flooding forth in the obvious yet grand metaphor a page later, when poor Louisa closes her hand, as if upon a graspable reality, and slowly opens it to disclose that her heart, like that of Tennyson's protagonist in *Maud,* is a handful of dust.

That is the true, dark power of *Hard Times.* Transcending Dickens's social vision, or his polemic for imagination, is his naked return to the domain of the drives, Eros and Death. The novel ends with an address to the reader that necessarily is far more equivocal than Dickens can have intended:

> Dear Reader! It rests with you and me, whether, in our two
> fields of action, similar things shall be or not. Let them be!
> We shall sit with lighter bosoms on the hearth, to see the ashes
> of our fires turn grey and cold.

Presumably, our imaginative escape from Gradgrindism into poetry will lighten our bosoms, even as we watch the reality principle overtake us. But the power of Dickens's rhetoric is in those gray and cold ashes, handfuls of dust that gather everywhere in the pages of *Hard Times.* Gradgrind, or the world without imagination, fails as a satire upon Utilitarianism, but triumphs frighteningly as a representation of the drive beyond the pleasure principle.

The Industrial Novels:
Hard Times

Raymond Williams

> Ordinarily Dickens's criticisms of the world he lives in are casual and incidental — a matter of including among the ingredients of a book some indignant treatment of a particular abuse. But in *Hard Times* he is for once possessed by a comprehensive vision, one in which the inhumanities of Victorian civilization are seen as fostered and sanctioned by a hard philosophy, the aggressive formulation of an inhumane spirit.

This comment by F. R. Leavis on *Hard Times* serves to distinguish Dickens's intention from that of Mrs Gaskell in *Mary Barton. Hard Times* is less imaginative observation than an imaginative judgement. It is a judgement of social attitudes, but again it is something more than *North and South*. It is a thorough-going and creative examination of the dominant philosophy of industrialism — of the hardness that Mrs Gaskell saw as little more than a misunderstanding, which might be patiently broken down. That Dickens could achieve this more comprehensive understanding is greatly to the advantage of the novel. But against this we must set the fact that in terms of human understanding of the industrial working people Dickens is obviously less successful than Mrs Gaskell: his Stephen Blackpool, in relation to the people of Mary Barton, is little more than a diagrammatic figure. The gain in comprehension, that is to say, has been

From *Culture and Society 1780-1950.* © 1958 by Raymond Williams. Columbia University Press, 1958.

achieved by the rigours of generalization and abstraction; *Hard Times* is an analysis of Industrialism, rather than experience of it.

The most important point, in this context, that has to be made about *Hard Times* is a point about Thomas Gradgrind. Josiah Bounderby, the other villain of the piece, is a simple enough case. He is, with rough justice, the embodiment of the aggressive money-making and power-seeking ideal which was a driving force of the Industrial Revolution. That he is also a braggart, a liar and in general personally repellent is of course a comment on Dickens's method. The conjunction of these personal defects with the aggressive ideal is not (how much easier things would be if it were) a necessary conjunction. A large part of the Victorian reader's feelings against Bounderby (and perhaps a not inconsiderable part of the twentieth-century intellectual's) rests on the older and rather different feeling that trade, as such, is gross. The very name (and Dickens uses his names with conscious and obvious effect), incorporating *bounder,* incorporates this typical feeling. The social criticism represented by *bounder* is, after all, a rather different matter from the question of aggressive economic individualism. Dickens, with rough justice, fuses the separate reaction, and it is easy not to notice how one set of feelings is made to affect the other.

The difficulty about Thomas Gradgrind is different in character. It is that the case against him is so good, and his refutation by experience so masterly, that it is easy for the modern reader to forget exactly *what* Gradgrind is. It is surprising how common is the mistake of using the remembered name, Gradgrind, as a class-name for the hard Victorian employer. The valuation which Dickens actually asks us to make is more difficult. Gradgrind is a Utilitarian: seen by Dickens as one of the *feeloosofers* against whom Cobbett thundered, or as one of the *steam-engine intellects* described by Carlyle. This line is easy enough, but one could as easily draw another: say, Thomas Gradgrind, Edwin Chadwick, John Stuart Mill. Chadwick, we are told, was "the most hated man in England," and he worked by methods, and was blamed for "meddling," in terms that are hardly any distance from Dickens's Gradgrind. Mill is a more difficult instance (although the education of which he felt himself a victim will be related, by the modern reader, to the Gradgrind system). But it seems certain that Dickens has Mill's *Political Economy* (1849) very much in mind in his general indictment of the ideas which built and maintained Coketown. (Mill's reaction, it may be noted, was the expressive "that creature Dickens.") It is easy now to realize that Mill was something more than a Gradgrind. But we are missing Dickens's point if we fail to see that in condemning Thomas Gradgrind, the representative figure, we are invited also to condemn the kind of thinking and the methods of enquiry and legislation which in fact promoted a large measure of social and industrial reform. One wonders, for example, what a typical Fabian feels when he is invited to condemn Gradgrind, not as an individual but as a type. This may, indeed, have something to do with the common error of memory about Gradgrind to which I have referred. Public commission, Blue Books, Parliamentary legislation — all these, in the world of *Hard Times* — are Gradgrindery.

For Dickens is not setting Reform against Exploitation. He sees what we normally understand by both as two sides of the same coin, Industrialism. His positives do not lie in social improvement, but rather in what he sees as the elements of human nature — personal kindness, sympathy, and forbearance. It is not the model factory against the satanic mill, nor is it the humanitarian experiment against selfish exploitation. It is, rather, individual persons against the System. In so far as it is social at all, it is the Circus against Coketown. The schoolroom contrast of Sissy Jupe and Bitzer is a contrast between the education, practical but often inarticulate, which is gained by living and doing, and the education, highly articulated, which is gained by systemization and abstraction. It is a contrast of which Cobbett would have warmly approved; but in so far as we have all (and to some extent inevitably) been committed to a large measure of the latter, it is worth noting again what a large revaluation Dickens is asking us to make. The instinctive, unintellectual, unorganized life is the ground, here, of genuine feeling, and of all good relationships. The Circus is one of the very few ways in which Dickens could have dramatized this, but it is less the Circus that matters than the experience described by Sleary:

> that there ith a love in the world, not all Thelf-interetht after all, but thomething very different . . . it hath a way of ith own of calculating or not calculating, which thomehow or another ith at leatht ath hard to give a name to, ath the wayth of the dogth ith.

It is a characteristic conclusion, in a vitally important tradition which based its values on such grounds. It is the major criticism of Industrialism as a whole way of life, and its grounds in experience have been firm. What is essential is to recognize that Dickens saw no social expression of it, or at least nothing that could be "given a name to." The experience is that of individual persons. Almost the whole organization of society, as Dickens judges, is against it. The Circus can express it because it is not part of the industrial organization. The Circus is an end in itself, a pleasurable end, which is instinctive and (in certain respects) anarchic. It is significant that Dickens has thus to go outside the industrial situation to find any expression of his values. This going outside is similar to the Canada in which *Mary Barton* ends, or the legacy of Margaret Hale. But it is also more than these, in so far as it is not only an escape but a positive assertion of a certain kind of experience, the denial of which was the real basis (as Dickens saw it) of the hard times.

It was inevitable, given the kind of criticism that Dickens was making, that his treatment of the industrial working people should have been so unsatisfactory. He recognizes them as objects of pity, and he recognizes the personal devotion in suffering of which they are capable. But the only conclusion he can expect them to draw is Stephen Blackpool's:

Aw a muddle!

This is reasonable, but the hopelessness and passive suffering are set against the attempts of the working people to better their conditions. The trade unions are dismissed by a stock Victorian reaction, with the agitator Slackbridge. Stephen Blackpool, like Job Legh, is shown to advantage because he will not join them. The point can be gauged by a comparison with Cobbett, whose criticism of the System is in many ways very similar to that of Dickens, and rests on so many similar valuations, yet who was not similarly deceived, even when the trade unions came as a novelty to him. The point indicates a wider comment on Dickens's whole position.

The scathing analysis of Coketown and all its works, and of the supporting political economy and aggressive utilitarianism, is based on Carlyle. So are the hostile reactions to Parliament and to ordinary ideas of reform. Dickens takes up the hostility, and it serves as a comprehensive vision, to which he gives all his marvellous energy. But his identification with Carlyle is really negative. There are no social alternatives to Bounderby and Gradgrind: not the time-serving aristocrat Harthouse; not the decayed gentlewoman Mrs Sparsit; nowhere, in fact, any active Hero. Many of Dickens's social attitudes cancel each other out, for he will use almost any reaction in order to undermine any normal representative position. *Hard Times,* in tone and structure, is the work of a man who has "seen through" society, who has found them all out. The only reservation is for the passive and the suffering, for the meek who shall inherit the earth but not Coketown, not industrial society. This primitive feeling, when joined by the aggressive conviction of having found everyone else out, is the retained position of an adolescent. The innocence shames the adult world, but also essentially rejects it. As a whole response, *Hard Times* is more a symptom of the confusion of industrial society than an understanding of it, but it is a symptom that is significant and continuing.

Dickens's *Hard Times:*
The Romance as Radical Literature

Robert E. Lougy

Hard Times has been praised for its humanistic intentions, criticized for its deplorable execution, and laid to rest, alongside *Diana of the Crossways* and *Felix Holt,* in those grounds reserved for the lesser creations of great authors. If *Hard Times* were, as one critic has suggested, "one of [Dickens's] dullest and least successful works," interment would indeed be an act of kindness. If, however, the fault lies less with *Hard Times* than with the manner in which it has been regarded, what is called for is not a premature act of literary euthanasia, but a new look at the work itself. Previously read and judged in comparison with Dickens's other novels, *Hard Times* has not, to put it gently, fared very well. It seems to collapse under the sheer weight of F. R. Leavis's "great tradition" and does not do much better even when judged by the less demanding modern criteria we usually bring to bear upon the novel. Its characters seem unbelievable in their exaggerated traits of goodness and evil, its plot wooden and mechanical, and its moral vision and artistic resolution less than satisfying.

However, Northrop Frye suggested some time ago that a "more relative and Copernican view must take [the] place" of the "[Ptolemaic] novel-centered view of prose fiction," and *Hard Times*'s critical fate is a case in point of what happens when a Ptolemaic system, as it were, is imposed upon a work operating in accordance with different laws. Our understanding and appreciation of *Hard Times* are diminished if we ask of it the same things we ask, for example, of *Great Expectations. Great*

From *Dickens Studies Annual,* vol. 2, edited by Robert B. Partlow, Jr. ©1979 by AMS Press, Inc.

Expectations is undoubtedly one of Dickens's finest novels; *Hard Times,* on the other hand, is not a novel, but a romance and operates, as Hawthorne long ago pointed out, according to inherently different laws. But although it is a romance, *Hard Times* is at the same time unique as a romance for several reasons: first, one of its major themes is, in fact, the death of romance; and secondly, there is internal evidence, especially in the character of Stephen Blackpool, of Dickens's attempts to remain within the novel tradition and its nineteenth-century brand of social realism. When Dickens finally does depart from the novel form, he neither falsifies nor simplifies an originally sound idea, but yields instead to a truer vision that thwarts his attempts to deny it.

Hard Times operates primarily within psychological rather than social categories and the issues it raises are directed less to the question of how man can create a more generous and humane society than to the question of whether society is not by definition corrupt and inhumane. The nature of the questions *Hard Times* raises makes it a radical work, one whose radicalism is seen most clearly when Dickens tries to come to terms with a question implicit throughout it — namely, what must man do to be saved. It is in his attempt to cope with this question that Dickens moves toward the romance, since it, for reasons suggested by Northrop Frye, offered him a particular creative freedom the novel form could not have provided. As Frye observes,

> the essential difference between novel and romance lies in the conception of characterization. The romancer does not attempt to create "real people" so much as stylized figures which expand into psychological archetypes. . . . That is why the romance so often radiates a glow of subjective intensity that the novel lacks, and why a suggestion of allegory is constantly creeping in around its fringes. Certain elements of character are released in the romance which make it naturally a more revolutionary form than the novel.
>
> *(Anatomy of Criticism)*

Dickens turned, as it were, toward a potentially revolutionary form within which to accommodate what is in many ways his most radical piece of writing.

In order to understand *Hard Times* more fully, however, we need to go back to an essay published four months prior to the time Dickens began working on *Hard Times,* for in it Dickens presents the essential germs of that vision of man's psychic and imaginative life he was later to dramatize, develop, and enrich in *Hard Times.* Two months after completing *Bleak House,* Dickens published in *Household Words* a short essay, "Frauds on the Fairies," in which he attacked George Cruikshank's editorial bowdlerizing of a volume of fairy tales. The essay is important, however, not for what it reveals either about Cruikshank or fairy tales per se, but for what it reveals about Dickens's own attitudes toward the role of art in man's life. His "very great tenderness for the fairy literature of our childhood" arises from the capacity of such literature "to keep us, in some sense, ever young, by preserving through our worldly ways one slender track not overgrown with weeds, where we may walk with children, sharing their delights." This small imaginative plot, the "fairy flower garden," is threatened by the intrusion of the adult consciousness, the "Whole Hog of unwieldy dimensions," which can destroy the joy or "delight" that energizes the poetic imagination. Once this imaginative power is lost, man is isolated from his past and the fragmenting and dehumanizing process Dickens sees inherent in industrial civilization is accelerated. The essay's language seems excessive in places until one realizes that Dickens is concerned with much more than merely the bowdlerizing of a single edition of fairy tales. When Dickens writes, for example, that "it is a *matter of grave importance* that Fairy tales should be respected" (italics mime), he means precisely what he says, for in them he finds not only a literary tradition, but an answer to the question of how man is to be saved.

The fairy tale's "grave importance" lies in its capacity to act as a mediating force between man and the phenomenal world and in its ability to substantively transform that relationship. By reuniting man to his past, the fairy tale makes it possible for him to become transfigured by the artistic and imaginative power created by the emotions of joy and wonder. Conversely, isolation from the past and its childhood emotions results in the fate of a Josiah Bounderby, a man committed to the ethos of death and trapped within a diseased imagination. While in Pegasus' Arms, an inn significantly named after the symbol of the poetic imagination, Bounderby is warned by one of the circus people to "give it [his philosophy] mouth in your own building . . . because this [the inn] isn't a strong building, and too much of you might bring it down!" (book 1, chap. 6). The Hog has only the power to destroy the flower garden; the garden, on the other hand, has the power to save the Hog from destroying itself. But if the imaginative power is to be redemptive, it must be nonuseful: it must resist compromise with the world of utility. "To preserve [the fairy tales] in their usefulness," Dickens writes, "they must be as much perserved in their simplicity, and purity, and innocent extravagance, as if they were actual fact."

But in spite of its occasional flashes of insight, "Frauds on the Fairies" is by no means an aesthetic or philosophical essay. Its insights, however brilliant in spots, remain too brief and too scattered to support the weight of a sustained argument. Its importance, rather, lies in the fact that the issues it raises show up again four months later in *Hard Times,* some of them intact and some of them seriously modified. One of the most serious modifications is the way in which Dickens's attitude toward the relationship between art and society changes. In the essay, Dickens views the "fairy flower garden" and the "whole Hog" as uniquely different but not necessarily mutually exclusive and seems to suggest that man can keep them separate but still maintain a dual allegiance to each. *Hard Times,* too, seems to end on the note of a similar dual allegiance — Louisa Gradgrind as a teller of tales within the heart of Coketown — but the similarity is more apparent than real. "Frauds on the Fairies" can hold out hope because Dickens can still believe in society's ability to accommodate those human values embodied in fairy tale literature; in *Hard Times,* on the other hand, Dickens becomes more strident as he realizes the futility inherent in such a hope. *Hard Times* moves away from the earlier essay in that it finally denies and belies Dickens's attempts to suggest a possible amelioration of the conflicts inherent within it.

Hard Times's world is a world of romance gone mad. The fairy tale elements are present — castles, fairy palaces, serpents, giants, and dragons — but they have become parodies of an earlier imaginative world whose qualities they perversely mock. Its landscape, like the landscape of romance, is one of the mind, an external symbol of the psychic condition of its inhabitants. In this case, it is a death mask which serves to remind us of man's capacity to create a world conducive only to his own death and destruction.

> [Coketown] was a town of red brick, or of brick that would have been red if the smoke and ashes had allowed it; but as matters stood, it was a town of unnatural red and black, like the painted face of a savage. It was a town of machinery and tall chimneys, out of which interminable serpents of smoke trailed themselves for ever and ever, and never got uncoiled. It had a black canal in it, and a river that ran purple with ill-smelling dye, and vast piles of buildings full of windows where there was a rattling and a trembling all day long, and where

> the piston of the steam-engine worked monotonously up and
> down like the head of an elephant in a state of melancholy
> madness.
>
> (BOOK I, CHAP. 5)

Self-contained and virtually autonomous, it allows for little movement
beyond it. Few of its citizens depart, even fewer enter. Driven away
because he insisted on being a man as well as a "hand," Stephen
Blackpool was returning when death intervened between him and his
destination. James Harthouse, presented as a parody of the archetypal
tempter — a Lucifer "trimmed, smoothed, and varnished, according to
the mode . . . aweary of vice, and aweary of virtue" (book 2, chap. 8) —
is the only major character not affiliated with the circus to enter
Coketown from the outside, but even he carries with him a card of introduction from Tom Gradgrind, Sr., one of Coketown's most il-
lustrious citizens. Tom Gradgrind, Jr., is virtually dead before he
escapes from Coketown on a voyage during which he will complete his
death. He was, we read, "horribly fevered, bit his nails down to the
quick, spoke in a hard rattling voice, and with lips that were black and
burnt up" (book 3, chap. 4).

Similarly, the nonhuman elements in Coketown are isolated from
external forces and powers. Threatened by the natural forces of life,
Coketown assures itself of survival by moving toward a deathlike stasis.
Its success is almost complete, but the city still finds antagonists in the
powers of the sun and rain. The sun, however, is vanquished by
Coketown: appearing for only one-half hour each day, "eternally in
eclipse, through a medium of smoked glass" (book 2, chap. 6), it is
unable to fight off those high chimneys which conceal it by "puffing out
poisonous volumes" of smoke and gas. Coketown's final success is seen
in the conversion of its major antagonist to its cause:

> The sun itself, however beneficent generally, was less kind to
> Coketown than hard frost, and rarely looked intently into any
> of its closer regions without engendering more death than
> life. So does the eye of Heaven itself become an evil eye, when
> incapable or sordid hands are interposed between it and the
> things it looks upon to bless.
>
> (BOOK 2, CHAP. I)

Against the power of the rain, the forces of Coketown are less triumphant: "the rain fell, and the Smoke-serpents submissive to the curse of

all that tribe, trailed themselves upon the earth" (book 1, chap. 11). But since the powers of death have already gained control of Coketown's inhabitants, the city's unnatural forces can tolerate the minor threats posed by nature without fearing any major defeat. Coketown's factories and machines continually reassert their power by diminishing the power of life. The energy they represent is a constant factor: it can be apportioned out in equal or unequal degrees, but it can be neither increased nor decreased. By making use of this natural law in an otherwise unnatural environment, Coketown has created a domain in which human energy is displaced, drained from the humans and converted into machinery which becomes, in turn, heavily energized and anthropomorphized.

> The atmosphere of those Fairy palaces was like the breath of the simoom: and their inhabitants, wasting with heat, toiled languidly in the desert. But no temperature made the melancholy mad elephants [the steam engines] more mad or more sane.
>
> (BOOK 2, CHAP. I)

Throughout the work, we discover within the larger strata of Coketown's society the operation of psychological principles which, in turn, manifest themselves in a civilization that at once reflects and determines their shape. Consequently, it is impossible to speak of *Hard Times*'s outer world without simultaneously speaking of the inner world of its inhabitants, for Coketown is but the collective symbol of a people reduced to deadness and kept alive only to perpetuate this deadness.

> [Coketown was] inhabited by people equally like one another, who all went in and out at the same hours, with the same sound upon the same pavements, to do the same work, and to whom every day was the same as yesterday and tomorrow, and every year the counterpart of the last and the next.
>
> (BOOK I, CHAP. 5)

Having created an environment that mirrors their own deadness and assures its continuity, Coketown's citizens are appropriately described by Dickens as automatons engaged in the repetition of meaningless acts within a world for which time no longer offers the possibility of growth and change. Coketown strangles all manifestations of sexuality and imagination — each an attribute of Eros, or life — and thereby weakens the only power that can oppose Thanatos, or death. Finally emerging as a pattern within *Hard Times* is a cycle whose implications are so far-reaching that even Freud, who was later to come across it, describes it with trepidation: namely, the more energy the citizens of Coketown expend upon industrialization (read "civilization"), the less energy they have to slow down their own ever-accelerating momentum toward death. Love (Eros, imagination, sexuality) alone can redeem man; yet love is the very thing civilization must repress if it is to survive. As Freud puts it,

> in the course of development [of civilization] the relation of love to civilization loses it ambiguity. On the one hand love comes into opposition to the interests of civilization; on the other, civilization threatens love with substantial restrictions.

The relation of *Hard Times*'s plot to Freud's major thesis in *Civilization and Its Discontents* becomes apparent if, in the above passage, we substitute "Stephen Blackpool" for "love" and "Bounderby" for "civilization." When we realize that Freud's statement both defines and describes one of *Hard Times*'s major conflicts, that allegory in romance spoken of earlier by Frye begins to assume in *Hard Times*'s case an ominous shape.

It is the appearance of this cycle that distinguishes *Hard Times* from Dickens's earlier works. A novel such as *Bleak House,* for example, can be read in part as Dickens's attempt to define and hopefully to alleviate particular social ills; *Hard Times,* on the other hand, dramatizes the futility of such an attempt. In his introduction to an edition of *Hard Times,* Shaw spoke of this essential difference:

> This [*Hard Times*] is Karl Marx, Carlyle, Ruskin, Morris, Carpenter, rising up against civilization itself as against a disease, and declaring that it is not our disorder but our order that is horrible; that it is not our criminals but our magnates that are robbing and murdering us; and that it is not merely Tom All Alone's that must be demolished and abolished, pulled down, rooted up . . . but our entire social system.

As Shaw suggests, Dickens previously sought to expose the "sins and wickednesses and follies of a great civilization," but in *Hard Times* he realized that "until Society is reformed, no man can reform himself." Once this realization occurred, Dickens's bonds with the nineteenth-century humanism of Coleridge are weakened to such an extent that a final severance seems inevitable. But for a man whose previous intellectual ties with this humanistic tradition were so strong, neither the realization nor the break could come easily.

The tension created in *Hard Times* by Dickens's moving away from this tradition is seen most clearly in the figure of Stephen Blackpool. Stephen's death marks the shift of power within *Hard Times* from a tradition that looked toward love and compassion as effectual powers of social change to Dickens's private vision of civilization per se as corrupt. Dickens creates in Stephen Blackpool a character who almost alone in *Hard Times* embodies the struggle of an individual against a dehumanizing society and then can find nothing to do with him but kill him. Stephen's two major conflicts — with his wife and with Bounderby — are but two sides of the same coin, and his failure to solve either suggests the powerlessness of love in modern civilization. For his effort to free himself from the dead, and deadening, relationship with his wife is thwarted by the same powers that forbade Stephen from asserting his individuality, punished him when he did so, and ultimately created circumstances that precipitated his death. *Hard Times*'s critics have so readily given their assent to Ruskin's description of Stephen, "a dramatic perfection, instead of a characteristic example of an honest workman," that they have failed to observe that even Stephen does not escape Coketown's blight. Coketown is characterized by aggression — man against nature, nature against man, man against man, and man against himself — and Stephen, too, participates in it. The pain arising from the first conflict results in an outward aggression (the barely averted murder of his wife), while the second leads to an inward aggression (his passive response to the inequities leveled against him and his almost active acceptance of death when it finally comes).

The difficulty that Dickens confronts in his characterization of Stephen is not due to his falling back on facile or simplistic resolutions, although in part he does just this, but to his moving into a realm of experience previously unexplored by him. Stephen's protestations to Bounderby that love, kindness, humility, and patience could alone unite the rich and the poor gain their stridency from Dickens's urgent need to believe in what Stephen says. But behind these protestations is Stephen's and, by inference, Dickens's recognition that only death could end Stephen's problems. Seeing in this world neither clarity nor fulfillment — "Ah, Rachael, aw a muddle! Fro' first to last, a muddle" — Stephen quite early in the work seems to intuit the inadequacy of such virtues in alleviating social conditions and consequently looks for a final reconciliation between his dreams and reality in the world beyond.

> And so I will try t' look t' th' time, and so I will try t' trust t' th' time, when thou [Rachael] and me at last shall walk together

far awa', beyond the deep gulf, in th' country where thy little sister is.

(BOOK I, CHAP. 13)

When Stephen does die, his death scene appears pathetic at best and stock melodrama at worst. But within it we find evidence of the tension created by Dickens's characterization of Stephen. Stephen's death scene represents, as it were, a pyrrhic victory for Dickens's public voice in that it not only belies the work's stronger controlling vision, but comes precariously close to validating Marx's famous maxim about religion's opiate quality. The unwillingness on Dickens's part to follow the implications of Stephen's death through to the end is seen when he brings forth a resolution — namely, heavenly compensation for earthly suffering — similar to the one offered by a bulk of Evangelical literature written in defense of the status quo. But in spite of his attempts to soften the impact of Stephen's death, Dickens still shows us that in this world there is little room for love, goodness, and humility, and that the God of the poor is not much help to them while they are alive.

When viewed in this context, Dickens's comment that "I have done what I hope is a good thing with Stephen, taking his story as a whole," becomes, as its tone suggests, ambivalently correct. In two senses, what he does with Stephen is good. First, *Hard Times* demands Stephen's death since the conflict he embodies is incapable of any other resolution. The inclusion of a penitent industrialist, for example, such as is found in Mrs. Gaskell's *Mary Barton,* would have been out of place and would have falsified Dickens's vision in this work. Secondly, Stephen's death seems to suggest that in the nightmare world of Coketown, suffering does in fact end with death. And in a world where merely the attempt to assert one's individuality evokes such disasterous consequences, it is perhaps optimistic to assert that one can still die a human death. It is in this respect that *Hard Times* comes closest to Frye's sixth phase of satire, a vision that "differs from a pure inferno mainly in the fact that in human experience suffering has an end in death." In a profounder sense, however, what Dickens does with Stephen is anything but good. He creates a good and gentle man, bestows upon him the task of fighting, armed only with individual goodness, an inhuman social system, and then cannot find a way to keep him alive. Stephen's literal death is demanded by his earlier expulsion from Coketown. His guilt or innocence in the robbery is irrelevant: even if he had been exonerated of the crime, the best Stephen could have hoped for would have been readmission to a society which still would have denied him his freedom and individuality.

Stephen Blackpool can be viewed on another level as the proletarian hero of a work whose implications finally become too large for him to carry. As a proletarian hero, Stephen possesses the characteristics of the pastoral hero as well: he is innocent and uneducated, but endowed with common sense and a rustic eloquence. As Empson points out, both pastoral and proletarian art "attempt to reconcile some conflict between the parts of a society"—in *Hard Times,* between employer (Bounderby) and employee (Stephen Blackpool)—and depend upon the individual's ability to transcend artificial social gulfs for this reconciliation. The shepherd is either a real aristocrat in disguise or is gifted with an aristocratic soul; the worker is able to reach the employer on human and thus genuine terms: Stephen's last major confrontation with Bounderby (book 2, chap. 5) is a classic example of such an attempt. In so far as both assume the possibility of such a breakthrough, they are optimistic; and, in part, their optimism depends upon the absence of any final restraint of man's capacity to effect such change. But it is precisely toward this final restraint that the dialectic established within *Hard Times* seems to point. *Hard Times* moves primarily within psychological rather than social categories and ultimately suggests a dialectic more akin to the life-death axis of Freud's *Civilization and Its Discontents* than to the employer-employee axis of the proletarian art. The battle waged in *Hard Times* is not between labor and capital, but between Eros and Thanatos, and consequently, the possibility of Stephen effecting meaningful change is denied. Stephen Blackpool remains, as Dickens's own comment about him implies, an anomaly in *Hard Times,* both for Bounderby, the employer who must fire him, and for Dickens, the artist who must kill him.

The creation of Stephen Blackpool, however, was but one of the problems *Hard Times* posed for Dickens. Dickens's letters attest to the fact that the work was in many ways an exceptionally difficult piece for him to write, primarily because, as Dickens describes it, of its lack of that "elbow room" his previous fiction had provided. It is, however, hard to accept this reason as the sole cause. By 1854 Dickens was an experienced novelist and journalist and had undoubtedly confronted the "difficulty of space" before. Also, the language used by Dickens to describe the agony involved the writing *Hard Times* would itself suggest that the trouble was located deeper than Dickens's own diagnosis implies. Dickens most likely did find it tasking to work on a cameo when he had been used to working on murals, but another reason for his difficulty lies, I think, in the dual directions he found his creative energies moving:

toward the book his dedication of *Hard Times* to Carlyle suggests he wanted to write, and toward the book he was in fact writing. His own statements about *Hard Times,* his condition of mind (and body) when he completed it, and the difficulties within the piece itself suggest that *Hard Times* became for Dickens much more than a dramatized version of the maxim, "All work and no play makes Jack a dull boy."

The work's other major characters, Bounderby, Gradgrind, and Sissy Jupe, invite criticism almost as much as Blackpool himself. None of them would survive in a realistic novel attempting to depict through "plausible characterization" various conflicts on social and personal levels. But such a novel, on the other hand, would necessarily be a tame venture compared to *Hard Times.* What gives *Hard Times* its power is neither its plausibility nor its verisimilitude, but rather the presence within it of those qualities of romance Frye speaks of: the expansion of "stylized figures" into "psychological archetypes," and the release of those "certain elements of character" which make the romance "naturally a more revolutionary form than the novel." Dickens's *Hard Times* attacks nothing less than the reality principle itself; and consequently, plausibility and verisimilitude become questionable criteria by which to judge it.

Those characters in *Hard Times* who sustain Dickens's vision do so by first violating our usual expectations of how people act and then carrying us to the truths that lie in front of our expectations. Bounderby and Louisa Gradgrind are woven together by a psychic condition that finds its poetic logic in the imagery of fire and enclosure. Fire is alluded to throughout: the steam engines, the heat that bakes the city and its citizens, Tom Gradgrind, Jr., horribly fevered with lips "black and burnt up," and the fireplace in front of which his sister sits. The imagery of enclosure is equally pervasive: the self-contained, autonomous world of Coketown itself, its walls and narrow streets, its castles, banks, palaces, mine shafts, factories, coalpits, and again Louisa Gradgrind's fireplace. This poetic logic is in turn reinforced by Dickens's narrative logic, episodes and authorial observation. Two comments in particular from the works's narrative fiber make it clear how Dickens, prefiguring twentieth-century studies of fire imagery such as Freud's study of the Promethean myth and [Gaston] Bachelard's *The Psychoanalysis of Fire,* lands upon highly effective symbols to contain and illuminate the work's controlling theme: the consequences of the repression of man's sexuality and imagination. The first comment, Dickens's observation that the ghost of a strangled imagination manifests itself in the form of groveling sensualities (book 2, chap. 3), reveals Bounderby with a clarity that neither poetic nor narrative logic could have individually achieved. The second, "all closely imprisoned forces rend and destroy," allows us to see Louisa Gradgrind—her relationship to her brother and to Bounderby and her meditations before the fireplace—as a total character. Two of the major life-forces of Eros, sexuality (Dickens's "closely imprisoned forces") and imagination (his "strangled imagination"), are repressed, and their repression gives rise to a sickness whose cure lies not in the eradication of society's ills, but in the eradication of society itself.

In many respects Bounderby embodies that paradox that goes by the name of civilization. He is at once both its victim and its perpetrator. Grossly sensual, he is also an archetype of impotence; intensely contemptuous of anything bordering on the imaginative, he has erected his life upon a huge fiction; a blatantly aggressive and hard-nosed industrialist, he remains throughout a man-child, finding in Mrs. Sparsit the mother he has disavowed and the mistress he cannot have. He creates his life around the middle class's favorite myth pattern—the hero's rise from obscurity and poverty by means of enterprise, ingenuity, and sacrifice (e.g., Dick Whittington, the Horatio Alger myth, and the fairy tale, *Puss in the Boots*)—only to become one of literature's oldest stock figures of ridicule, the man bullied or dominated by women. In describing the sexual nature of Bounderby's frustration, Dickens remains sufficiently allusive to satisfy the publishing mores of Victorian England while at the same time leaving us with few doubts as to how we are to read his character. For example, the first time we meet Bounderby we confront

> a man with a great puffed head and forehead, swelled veins in his temples, and such a strained skin to his face that it seemed to hold his eyes open, . . . a man with a pervading appearance on him of being inflated like a balloon, and ready to start.
>
> (BOOK I, CHAP. 4)

Just after Louisa Gradgrind leaves him, following a brief and unconsummated marriage, the

> blustrous Bounderby crimsoned and swelled to such an extent . . . that he seemed to be, and probably was, on the brink of a fit. With his very ears a bright purple shot with crimson, he pent up his indignation.
>
> (BOOK 3, CHAP. 3)

The above passages must be among the most explicit allusions to sexual frustration in legitimate Victorian fiction. Dickens's metaphor may be a bit confused, but his message is clear enough.

Dickens's "Frauds on the Fairies" provides additional insight into the relationship between Bounderby's psychic condition, externalized in his physiognomy, and his fiction about his past. In it, Dickens suggests, as I have mentioned, that man's remembrance of his childhood literature allows him to "walk with children" and to share the child's joy in being part of the natural world. This joy, because it increases the strength of Eros, is a potentially liberating power; but in order to participate in it, man must deny those forces pressuring him into the abandonment of his childhood values and affirm the pleasure principle, the controlling force of the child and the artist. Coming close to Shelley's revolutionary concept of Eros, Dickens seems to imply that this quest must become a way of life not only for the artist, but for all men.

Looking at Bounderby in this light, we can see that he is the antiartist and that his fable about his youth in antiart. The artist is he who refuses to succumb to those attempts to sever him from his childhood, and his art derives from the tension between his fidelity to the natural and joyous reality of childhood and the contemporary pressures threatening this reality. Bounderby, on the other hand, has attempted to kill his childhood by destroying all his links with it and, in doing so, has replaced it with a fiction that affirms rather than denies the existing order. Childhood and art are redemptive insofar as they refuse to conform to the reality principle; Bounderby's fictionalized past arises out of an adult mind wholly attuned to the values of an industrialized society and thus is a binding rather than a liberating force. What society wants Bounderby and every man to become and what Bounderby envisions himself to be are inextricably merged. He is in this respect a perfect example of Marcuse's modern man who absorbs "societal authority" into his own conscience and unconscious until he believes he "lives his repression 'freely' as his own life" *(Eros and Civilization)*. But as Marcuse points out, this "freedom" is gained at a very high cost.

On one level, the cost levied against Bounderby is similar to that levied against Dickens's heroes who deny their past. Like Pip, Bounderby learns that the past invariably reveals itself, and that once revealed it destroys the fictional or illusory present. In *Hard Times,* the past is united to the present by Bounderby's mother, Mrs. Pegler, who, in keeping with the romance motif, comes across as a hybrid between an unwitting Fury and a more conventional English witch. "An old woman who

seems to have been flying into town on a broomstick, every now and
then" (book 2, chap. 8), Bounderby's mother revenges the crime of
matricide, i.e., his refusal to acknowledge her existence, after having
been thrust upon him by Mrs. Sparsit, the primary agent of Bounderby's
nemesis. "The spectacle of a matron [Mrs. Sparsit] of classical deportment, seizing an ancient woman [Mrs. Pegler] by the throat, and haling
her into [Bounderby's] dwelling-house" attracts, in turn, an unruly
chorus who

> closed in after Mrs. Sparsit and her prize; and the whole body
> made a disorderly eruption into Mr. Bounderby's dining-
> room, where the people behind lost not a moment's time in
> mounting on the chairs, to get the better of the people in
> front.
>
> (BOOK 3, CHAP. 5)

In one of *Hard Times*'s most brilliant strokes, Bounderby's public fable
about his past is destroyed in a spectacle during which a privately con-
cealed past is brought forth for public inspection.

Bounderby pays a greater price, however, than simply the loss of a
falsely gained reputation. By creating a concept of self that corresponds
to the industrial ethos around him, Bounderby is assimilated into that
ethos. As a consequence, he becomes a projection of his own antifan-
tasies, an embodiment of that aura of death he is helping to create. He is
Dickens's modern figure of death, no longer the Middle Age's skeletal
figure in dark robes, but the opulent and corpulent bureaucrat imposing
upon an outside world the death he carries within. Mrs. Sparsit, as
astute as she is evil, seems to see this death within Bounderby: "There
were occasions when in looking at him she was involuntarily moved to
shake her head, as who would say, 'Alas poor Yorick!'" (book 2, chap.
8). Bounderby's quest to make reality over in his own image results in his
destruction of all that with which he comes into contact. Louisa, Tom
Gradgrind, Blackpool, his other employees — everything and everyone he
touches, with the exception of Mrs. Sparsit — is immediately tainted with
death.

Mrs. Sparsit survives because she represents a force even stronger
than Bounderby. She is Dickens's version of Robert Graves's "capricious
and all-powerful Threefold Goddess, . . . mother, bride, and layer-out."
If, as Graves suggests, "the test of a poet's vision . . . is the accuracy of his
portrayal of the White Goddess and of the island over which she rules,"
then *Hard Times* belongs precisely where Leavis has put it, with "formally

poetic works." A highly connected "matron of classical deportment," Mrs. Sparsit is the work's fallen goddess. She moves with almost supernatural ease, "as if she had been caught up in a cloud and whirled away," among people and among "worms, snails, and slugs." She is Bounderby's harsh mother, his jealous bride, and in bringing about his downfall, his layer-out. Since she has fallen into a world, however, that renders individual goodness and individual evil equally ineffectual, her plans are but partially successful. It is not wholly her fault that she cannot carry her plans to their full fruition: *Hard Times's* world is a jealous one and has no room for either heroes or fallen goddesses.

Louisa Gradgrind, the intended victim of Mrs. Sparsit's machinations, is Bounderby's antagonist throughout *Hard Times,* yet shares much in common with him. While Bounderby is a man-child who has killed his childhood by his capitulation to the world of death around him, Louisa is a woman whose life has been broken by the absence of a childhood within it. Because she has never known those emotions of joy and wonder that create a connection between one's past and present, Louisa gazes into a fireplace only to discover the absence of that internal energy which makes growth possible. In front of a fireplace, Louisa resembles Bachelard's man engaged in reverie, "the man concerned with inner depths, a man in the process of development," and the man involved in "sexual reverie." She is, in other words, the artist concerned with the life-forces of imagination and sexuality. Her development, however, stops at an intellectual cognizance of her life's inadequacies, for her emotional life is destroyed by the absence of a childhood in the same way Bounderby's denial of his childhood destroys his.

> Neither, as she approached her old home now, did any of the best influences of old home descend upon her. The dreams of childhood—its airy fables; its graceful, beautiful, humane, impossible adornments of the world beyond: so good to be believed in once, so good to be remembered when outgrown, for then the least among them rises to the stature of a great Charity in the heart, suffering little children to come into the midst of it, and to keep with their pure hands a garden in the stony ways of this world, . . . simple and trustful, and not worldly-wise—what had she to do with these?
>
> (BOOK 2, CHAP. 9)

The language of this passage is almost identical to Dickens's description of the powers of childhood in his "Frauds on the Fairies" and suggests the extent to which Louisa Gradgrind embodies that fate Dickens saw in store for a world overrun by the "Whole Hog." She is the potential artist thwarted by a world inimical to imaginative powers, living proof of how the "closely imprisoned forces" of Eros rend and destroy. Bounderby is by no means exceptionally astute, but even he notes that "there are qualities in Louisa which — which have been harshly neglected and — and a little perverted" (book 3, chap. 3). Her passivity regarding her marriage to Bounderby, her dalliance with James Harthouse, the sexual overtones of her relationship with her brother, and her psychological and physical barrenness — all point toward the permanently damaging effects of Coketown upon an imaginative and sensitive person. Louisa Gradgrind is compassionate, wise, and loving; but the world in which she lives turns her compassion into a tool for evil, oppresses her wisdom in the name of reason, and first perverts her love and then renders it impotent.

Hard Times moves toward a world dominated by the forces of death. Within it, life exists precariously at best and is eventually either destroyed or made helpless. For this reason, Dickens chooses to keep the circus, the work's symbol of life, outside of Coketown's environs. John Holloway has noted that Dickens's "alternative [to Coketown] was something which lay altogether outside the major realities of the social situation with which he dealt" and sees this as evidence, in part, that *Hard Times* "operated (for all its obvious common sense and its genuine value) at a relatively shallow level of consciousness." It is, however, precisely Dickens's recognition of the "major realities of the social situation" that requires him to find Coketown's only alternative in the circus. For Coketown is not a world in which the forces of life and death coexist dialectically, but one in which Thanatos has an uncontested reign; thus, given this monistic nature of Coketown, the circus must remain on the town's perimeters. It may send emissaries to it (Sissy Jupe) and it can proffer help if approached (Tom Gradgrind's escape), but, if it is to survive, it must remain apart.

The circus is an omnipresent contradiction and repudiation of Coketown. It is, as Bounderby describes it, "queer sort of company, too, for a man who has raised himself" (book 1, chap. 6). He views it as a world of idleness and, in one respect, he is correct. It is a world of play, but play in the sense that Freud uses the term in speaking of the child and artist: it is a world rich in human experience, not because its citizens do not labor, but because their labor is nonrepressive and because their lives have remained faithful to the natural instincts of joy and love. Consequently the circus people are artists in the psychological sense that they assert themselves against the outside world dominated by reason and the reality principle. They neither produce, dominate, nor master; and thus Bounderby, who regards them as subversive, intuitively aligns himself with the reality principle. About the circus people, Dickens writes, "There was a remarkable gentleness and childishness about these people, a special inaptitude for any kind of sharp practice" (book 1, chap. 6). Marcuse, in speaking of Schiller's *An Aesthetical Education of Man,* describes "a genuinely humane civilization" as one in which "human existence will be play rather than toil, and man will live in display rather than need." What better symbol of such a humane world could Dickens have chosen? The circus people are children-artists by virtue of the life they lead — in their refusal to capitulate to Coketown's world and in their demand for a life of freedom and beauty.

In his essay on Dickens, Orwell observes that "even if Dickens was a bourgeois, he was certainly a subversive writer, a radical," not in his advocacy of change in the social structure, but in his advocacy of change of spirit.

> His radicalism is of the vaguest kind, and yet one always knows that it is there. . . . He has no constructive suggestions, not even a clear grasp of the nature of the society he is attacking, only an emotional perception that something is wrong.

But, as Orwell points out, such moral criticism can be every bit as revolutionary as political or economic criticism. Throughout much of his writings, Dickens realizes that certain evils cannot be removed so long as the present form of society exists; in *Hard Times,* however, he realizes that the problem is not the sickness of a particular society, but that society itself is a disease. On the one hand, there is the fairy flower garden, on the other, the Whole Hog whose *raison d'être* is the destruction of the garden — there is no middle ground between them. There is the circus and there is Coketown: how does one reconcile the two? Looking carefully at the conclusion of *Hard Times,* we can see, I think, that Dickens seeks such a reconciliation, but does not ultimately achieve it. The elder Gradgrind undergoes a change of heart (a device common to Victorian industrial novels, e.g., *Mary Barton* and *Alton Locke*), but only to become "therefore much despised by his late political associates" (book 3, chap. 9). In *Hard Times,* individual benevolence seems to be invariably accompanied by political impotence. Only Sissy Jupe, of all the work's major characters, seems to survive intact, probably for the reason that she is more among the world of Coketown than of it. An emissary from the circus, she provides a force for good that counters Mrs. Sparsit's force for evil, but both Sissy and Mrs. Sparsit finally have only a limited effect upon Coketown. Still, we read that Sissy is destined to bring children into this world and could regard this information as an optimistic note, as the inclusion of new life in an otherwise death-oriented world, were it not for the fact that when we anticipate the future lives of her children, we realize that the alternatives they will face as adults will still be Coketown on one hand and, hopefully, the circus on the other. We have no reason to believe that the structure of the society will have changed or that their psyches will be able to accommodate the dual allegiance Dickens hopes for in his essay, "Frauds on the Fairies," without suffering the same sort of damage Dickens has shown throughout *Hard Times*.

In yet another passage that appears toward the conclusion of *Hard Times,* Dickens—in depicting a scene reminiscent of Orwell's description of the Victorian novel's typical happy ending ("a vision of a huge, loving family of three or four generations, all crammed together in the same house and constantly multiplying, like a bed of oysters")—again seems to depart momentarily from the nightmare vision of Coketown:

> But, happy Sissy's happy children loving her [Louisa]; all children loving her; she, grown learned in childish lore; thinking no innocent and pretty fancy ever to be despised; trying hard to know her humbler fellow-creatures, and to beautify their lives of machinery and reality with those imaginative graces and delights, without which the heart of infancy will wither up, the sturdiest physical manhood will be morally stark death, and the plainest national prosperity figures can show will be the Writing on the Wall,—she holding this course as part of no fantastic vow, or bond, or brotherhood, or sisterhood, or pledge, or covenant, or fancy dress, or fancy fair; but simply as a duty to be done.
>
> (BOOK 3, CHAP. 9)

However, this passage, too, contains evidence of the tensions which run throughout *Hard Times*. On one hand, we see Dickens hoping to humanize an inhumane system without changing the system itself and, in doing so, mythicizing forces of social change such as the labor union into dark and diabolical organizations. In this respect, the passage is common middle-class fare and would have been acceptable to the staunchest defender of nineteenth-century capitalism.

But, on the other hand, Dickens finally expresses in unambiguous terms what previously the opposition between the circus and Coketown has demonstrated symbolically: the forces of life are specifically located within the domain of art (those "imaginative graces without which the heart of infancy will wither up, the sturdiest physical manhood will be morally stark death"), and the forces of death within civilization and reality ("their lives of machinery and reality"). In the usual sense, this is not a resolution, but merely another acknowledgment of the same problem we have seen in Dickens's refusal to bring the circus and Coketown together. When Dickens does try to convert this vision into social terms, the best he can do is to fall back upon a variation of what Orwell calls the "Good Rich Man" theme. Louisa Gradgrind, bestowing fairy tales among her "humbler fellow-creatures," becomes the granddaughter of Pickwick and the grandmother of *Our Mutual Friend*'s Boffin, the only real difference being that her male counterparts give money.

It is not surprising that Dickens has been criticized for failing to present a more meaningful solution. He moves through the fallen world of *Hard Times* only to arrive at what appears to be little more than a fairy godmother whose capacity for working miracles is extremely limited. But such a conclusion is not so simplistic as it seems, for what Dickens confronts is a dialectic which by its very nature denies a social solution. On one hand it is Orwell's dialectic between the moralist and the revolutionary (the former asserting that the social system cannot change until human nature changes, the latter denying that human nature can improve within a corrupt social system), but it is also the dialectic between Eros and Thanatos, between man's desire to live and his desire to die. At the conclusion of his *Civilization and Its Discontents,* Freud can only express the vague hope that Eros will somehow manage to assert itself against its immortal foe. Similarly, the conclusion of *Hard Times* will fail to satisfy us if we expect Dickens to turn for answers to where he has already looked, but found only emptiness.

Dickens cannot very well look to "machinery [either social or technological] and reality" for an answer—he has already identified them as the forces of death. The power they represent is finally impotent because the overwhelming problem facing man is one of a psychic rather than a social disorder. Since Coketown is but the manifestation of a collective psychic disorientation, any social restructuring can at best treat only the symptoms, not the cause, of society's sickness. It is possible that Dickens, by setting the circus on Coketown's perimeters, intended eventually to bring the two worlds together. Sissy Jupe's early entrance into Coketown seems to provide such a potential link; but when *Hard Times* ends, the circus and Coketown are as distant from one another as they were when it began. The circus remains an anarchic force, as evidenced by its final role in helping the younger Gradgrind to escape, and Coketown, on the other hand, remains secure, having successfully removed or isolated all potential threats to it.

But if Dickens looks neither to a change of heart from the industrialists nor to the usual social realities for a resolution, where then does he look? The question is difficult and perhaps even unfair, since we should not demand that Dickens provide us with an alternative to his vision, but only that his vision remain faithful to its own truths. However, I think that Dickens does approach, albeit in a tentative and groping manner, an alternative to the world of *Hard Times*. Dickens finally seems to be asking for a radical redefinition of man, of man whose heart is filled with charity in the revolutionary way Christ spoke of it or with love in the revolutionary way Shelley described it. And, for several reasons, such a redefinition of man, given the world Dickens presents in *Hard Times,* must occur independently of social process as we usually conceive of it. First of all, Coketown is inimical to progress: Dickens throughout makes it clear that Coketown's perpetuity depends upon a stasis it has virtually achieved. It is in this respect a world of death from which man must be reborn if he is to be saved. Blackpool recognizes this in his own muddled fashion and thus looks to the world beyond; Dickens recognizes it also, but hopes for a transformation that will take place on earth. Secondly a belief in social progress implies a faith in society's ability to set, as it were, its own house in order. But because, as Shaw puts it, Dickens's *Hard Times* sees society's sickness precisely in its order, any social reordering must by definition remain inadequate.

Finally, *Hard Times* points beyond social restructuring to the extent that it indicts not one particular society, but all societies and, in doing so, raises the question Empson sees in the most valuable works of art: "They carry an implication about the society they were written for; the question is whether the same must not be true of any human society, even if it is much better than theirs." Moving in *Hard Times* from proletarian to pastoral art, Dickens looks for a positive embodiment of values in a vision of what Marcuse has called the "aesthetic dimension," an artistically conceived world in which man's existence is beauty and his work play — in other words, Dickens's fairy flower garden and *Hard Times's* circus. Dimly seeing what Shelley sang of in *Prometheus Unbound,* Dickens seems to be asking for a world reborn and clothed in the beauty of Eros (love, charity, imagination). It is this power that gives the child possession of the world he views, it is this power that Dickens in his "Frauds on the Fairies" suggests our childhood literature can partially return to us, and it is only in this power that Dickens sees a way out of the nightmare world he has so vividly shown.

Such a change cannot come about, of course, either through man's reasoning or through the products of man's reason, the machinery of technocracy and bureaucracy. It begins and ends in the human heart and it is to the human heart that Dickens finally turns. Orwell has pointed out that this is often the direction in which Dickens looks:

> In every attack Dickens makes upon society he is always point-
> ing to a change of spirit rather than a change of structure. . . .
> Useless to change institutions without a "change of
> heart"—that, essentially, is what he is always saying.

But this same "change of heart" is also the final resort of novelists such as Mrs. Gaskell and Charles Kingsley and does not, in itself, distinguish a work such as *Hard Times* from other nineteenth-century industrial novels. In many respects, of course, Dickens is similar to his contemporaries in that he too is a bourgeois citizen who often looks upon the working classes and social ills with a fairly orthodox middle-class eye. His fear of the labor unions and his final reference to Rachael, "a woman working, ever working, but content and preferring to do it *as her natural lot*" (book 3, chap. 9, italics mine) attest to this.

But however middle class Dickens may have been and however many of its attitudes he might have shared, he also possessed that inexplicable greatness which we have chosen to call by the name of genius; and, in the case of *Hard Times,* this genius drove Dickens beyond the limits he probably envisioned. Dickens, the nineteenth-century citizen, would have denied the radical implications of *Hard Times,* but they are nevertheless present. Dickens as artist, in Plato's terms, dreams while awake and what his dreams reveal the fully awakened and nondreamer part of Dickens need not even fully understand or agree with. What ultimately matters is *Hard Times* itself. And it is, I think, a great work not in spite of, but because of its unevenness. For its unevenness arises from a conflict within Dickens himself and thus makes us spectators to the drama of artistic creation as well as to the drama that unfolds within *Hard Times*'s fictional world. *Hard Times* is a work of two voices: of the voice that wanted to keep Stephen Blackpool alive and of the stronger voice that realized that Stephen had to die, and these two voices are throughout in varying degrees of discord with one another.

Hard Times perhaps begins as a proletarian novel, but finally goes beyond the limits of proletarian art. More akin to the romance than the novel, it operates on psychological rather than social levels and is revolutionary in that it repudiates, by the very dialectics it establishes, that belief in progress and social amelioration to which another part of Dickens tenaciously clings. Dickens reaches through the art of *Hard Times* to a vision closer to Shelley's than to its dedicatee's, Thomas Carlyle, a vision whose final truth neither we nor Dickens can foretell, but one which we can deny only if we believe that our own Coketown has the energy and the desire to save itself.

Imagery and Theme in *Hard Times*

Robert Barnard

"I am afraid I shall not be able to get much here."

Dickens's disappointment in the Preston power-loom strike was obvious: the town was quiet, the people mostly sat at home, and there were no hints whatsoever from which he could work up one of his big set pieces. He would have been much happier, artistically, with something of a more French-revolutionary nature:

> I am in the Bull Hotel, before which some time ago the people assembled supposing the masters to be here, and on demanding to have them out were remonstrated with by the landlady in person. I saw the account in an Italian paper, in which it was stated that "the populace then environed the Palazzo Bull, until the padrona of the Palazzo heroically appeared at one of the upper windows and addressed them!" One can hardly conceive anything less likely to be represented to an Italian mind by this description, than the old, grubby, smoky, mean, intensely formal red brick house with a narrow gateway and a dingy yard, to which it applies.

One suspects Dickens would have liked to take the Italian view of the incident rather than the English. But he obviously felt there was nothing to

From *Imagery and Theme in the Novels of Dickens.*©1974 by the Norwegian Research Council for Science and the Humanities. Universitetsforlaget, 1974.

be done with industrial action as such: "I have no intention of striking," he wrote to Mrs. Gaskell. The decision changed not only the direction of the plot, but the whole tone and texture of the novel. If Dickens had found what he was hoping to find, the novel would surely have been at once more melodramatic and more "popular." As it is, the emotional key of the novel is low.

In most repects the decision was a fortunate one. At this period Dickens adopted the pusillanimous view that workers had a right to strike but were unwise to use that right, and his presentation would probably have been slanted as well as sensationalised. Dickens knew very little about the Northern industrial scene, and the North and the South are two nations. A brief visit was far from sufficient to understand the industrial worker and the stand he was taking. Again, in such a terse, compact novel the interest could not be widely diffused, and the comparative thinness of the Trade Union side of the novel enabled him to concentrate his attention relentlessly on the Hard Fact men (though even here Butt and Tillotson note that Dickens intended to establish an identity between the Gradgrind view of life and the "dandy," dilettante view, so roundly castigated in *Bleak House,* but was unable to find space for it).

Nevertheless, the discontent of the workers, and their banding together in Trade Unions could not be ignored altogether, and it is in the treatment of these themes that the reader is brought up against the major false note in the book. As many commentators have observed, the professional speaker from a nearby town whom Dickens saw addressing the striking workers during his visit to Preston becomes the Slackbridge of *Hard Times,* with the difference that in Preston the man was received with scant sympathy by the men, and was prevented from stirring up trouble by "the persuasive right hand of the chairman," whereas in *Hard Times* he gets a sympathetic hearing and brings about the ostracisation of Stephen.

The point is not as trivial as it might seem. Of course Dickens is under no obligation to be exact in his reporting; a misrepresentation of detail which allowed the better presentation of a wider truth about the industrial situation would have been understandable. But in this case Dickens makes the change in order to misrepresent the wider situation. Either to placate his middle-class readers, or else because a preconceived plotline forced the falsification on him, he depicts the workers as intelligent men misled by mischievous agitators—just the very line taken up towards the new Trade Unions by the fainthearted who baulked at offending either side. Edgar Johnson's heading for his chapter dealing with the writing of *Hard Times* — "The heaviest blow in my power" — is distinctly misleading. Dickens used the phrase in a letter written sixteen years before the visit to Preston. As far as the treatment of industrial unrest in this novel is concerned, the "blow" Dickens strikes is a muffled, misdirected one.

The importance of his misrepresentation of the situation is not merely extraliterary, for the falseness of Dickens's approach is quite evident in the text itself:

> As he stood there, trying to quench his fiery face with his drink of water, the comparison between the orator and the crowd of attentive faces turned towards him, was extremely to his disadvantage. Judging him by Nature's evidence, he was above the mass in very little but the stage on which he stood. In many great respects he was essentially below them. He was not so honest, he was not so manly, he was not so good-humoured; he substituted cunning for their simplicity, and passion for their safe solid sense. An ill-made, high-shouldered man, with lowering brows, and his features crushed into an habitually sour expression, he contrasted most unfavourably, even in his mongrel dress, with the great body of his hearers in their plain working clothes. Strange as it always is to consider any assembly in the act of submissively resigning itself to the dreariness of some complacent person, lord or commoner, whom three-fourths of it could, by no human means, raise out of the slough of inanity to their own intellectual level, it was particularly strange, and it was even particularly affecting, to see this crowd of earnest faces, whose honesty in the main no competent observer free from bias could doubt, so agitated by such a leader.
>
> (BOOK 2, CHAP. 4)

It does indeed appear strange; in fact nothing Dickens says can make it anything but inexplicable. Nor is he helped by the quality of his writing in the Trade Union section of the novel which at times ("no competent observer free from bias") resembles that of a leader-writer defending a distinctly dubious proposition.

The first consequence of making the workers malleable by such hands as Slackbridge is that Dickens's no doubt genuinely admiring descriptions of them and their attitudes no longer ring true. His comment that "age, especially when it strives to be self-reliant and cheerful, finds much consideration among the poor" sounds condescending, where similar tributes to the brick-makers' wives in *Bleak House* seem perfectly natural. Nor can one convincingly laud the intelligence of men who are persuaded by the eloquence of a windbag to persecute an admirable and unfortunate fellow-worker. And the second consequence is that, if he devalues and disowns the Trade Union movement, he is forced to look elsewhere for a panacea, since this is a novel which cries out for some sort of positive statement — seems in fact, almost to have presented itself to Dickens as the means of bringing his testimony on the subject to the public's notice. And thus he is forced into the drivelling fatuity of Stephen's "'dyin prayer that aw th'world may on'y coom toogether more, an' get a better unnerstan'in o' one another." Stated so baldly this message would be feeble in any industrial novel. In one that includes Bounderby it is patently ludicrous. Is it suggested that the "honest," "manly" and "good-humoured" workers should sort out their troubles amiably by getting together with this hectoring, lying bully? As far as the Trade Union section is concerned, this novel refutes its own thesis.

But in the parts of the novel concerning the Hard Fact men Dickens is much more at home. If the scenes involving Stephen and Rachael seem thinly written, superior padding, the Gradgrind-Bounderby scenes are hard-hitting and rich in layer upon layer of implication. The first impression these scenes give are of a powerful imagination holding itself in, of an almost painful discipline being exercised over an unruly creative urge. The descriptions of character are brief, forceful; the "keynotes" of the various sections are struck with admirable directness. Most of the chapters begin succinctly, even brutally: "Thomas Gradgrind, Sir. A man of realities. A man of facts and calculations"; or "The Gradgrind party wanted assistance in cutting the throats of the Graces." What would be matter for a page in Dickens's normal style is compressed to a three or four-line paragraph in the new, telegraphic style necessary for the short episodes of a weekly serial:

> Mr. James Harthouse began to think it would be a new sensation, if the face which changed so beautifully for the whelp, would change for him.
>
> (BOOK 2, CHAP. 7)

or

> I entertain a weak idea that the English people are as hard-worked as any people upon whom the sun shines. I acknowledge to this ridiculous idiosyncrasy, as a reason why

I would give them a little more play.

(BOOK I, CHAP. IO)

The idea that Dickens is a writer incapable of artistic self-control is a discredited one; no novel proves its untruth so well as this one. The letters of the time and the notes for the novel testify to the severity of the discipline which he kept himself under, but the reader also senses that he is consciously trying not to squeeze out entirely the exuberance and fluency of his mature style — hence the occasional latitude he allows himself in the depiction of, for example, the circus people and Bounderby.

Dickens's use of imagery in *Hard Times* is similarly spare, similarly effective. In the larger novels the aspects which acquire in the course of the novel symbolic overtones — be they weather, landscapes, buildings or whatever — are thoroughly, hauntingly established early on, and then subjected to elaboration and modification as the book progresses. The significance of the symbol, and the ramifications of that significance are gradually opened up to the reader; the emotional and intellectual effects that Dickens aims at are cumulative. No such technique was possible for *Hard Times*. There is nothing in this novel comparable to the prison in *Dorrit* or the river in *Our Mutual Friend*. Here Dickens's method is to strike a keynote, then remind the reader of it by constant repetition. For example, the keynote Coketown is struck in chapter 5 in three pages which suggest, with a wealth of illustrative example, emotional and imaginative repression, uniformity, spiritual death. The key features of the physical description are the "interminable serpents of smoke" from the chimneys and the piston of the steam-engine which looked like "the head of an elephant in a state of melancholy madness." Later, in chapter 10, we are told that from the express trains the lights in the factories made them look like fairy palaces. Whenever we need to be reminded of the emotional stagnation inherent in the Coketown system later in the book, Dickens simply mentions the serpent, the elephant and the fairy palaces, normally with no alteration or elaboration, none of the extravagances one might expect from him, given such material. Never has he made his points so economically.

A similar self-discipline is evident in the use of the staircase image, symbol of Louisa's gradual slipping into an adulterous relationship with Harthouse. It is first foreshadowed in chapter 7 of book 2, where Dickens mentions Louisa going "step by step, onward and downward, towards some end, yet so gradually, that she believed herself to remain motionless." Later we hear that she has fallen into a confidential alliance with Harthouse "by degrees so fine that she could not retrace them if she tried." By this time the image, and its usefulness in depicting a process which he himself had not space to trace in detail was clear to Dickens, and he decided to present the image as an authorial gift to Mrs. Sparsit:

> Now, Mrs. Sparsit was not a poetical woman; but she took an idea in the nature of an allegorical fancy, into her head. Much watching of Louisa, and much consequent observation of her impenetrable demeanour, which keenly whetted and sharpened Mrs. Sparsit's edge, must have given her as it were a lift, in the way of inspiration. She erected in her mind a mighty Staircase, with a dark pit of shame and ruin at the bottom; and down those stairs, from day to day and hour to hour, she saw Louisa coming.
>
> (BOOK 2, CHAP. 10)

From this point on Mrs. Sparsit becomes suitably single-minded in her idea until the moment when, she believes, Louisa "falls from the lowermost stair, and is swallowed up in the gulf." In the author's hand this image would have needed considerable elaboration and expansion; without that it would have seemed too rigid and unsympathetic as a symbol of the downward course of an unhappily married woman, desperately seizing the chance of a love she has never had, and would have suggested a too conventional moral judgement of her actions. As a figment of Mrs. Sparsit's imagination, however, it is perfect, and further develops the woman's combination of prurient curiosity and dreary respectability.

Hard Times is a reaffirmation of belief in fancy. Its targets are not Utilitarian or Political Economy, but some aspects of Utilitarianism, some results of Political Economy. The book is aimed, in fact, at all the tendencies of the age to repress the free creative imagination of men, to stifle their individuality, to make them cogs in a machine — mere numbers in a classroom, or "hands" without bodies or minds. That Dickens was unfair to Utilitarians, and in particular to their achievements in the great national cinder-heap, is only important if we agree with [Humphrey] House that Gradgrind is satirised as an "intellectual," that Dickens was taking on a philosophy. If this were true, then we might agree that he "did not understand enough of any philosophy even to be able to guy it successfully" (*The Dickens World*). But Utilitarianism plays the same role in Gradgrind's mind as, say, religion in Mrs. Clennam's: it acts as a formidable prop to traits of character which were formed quite independently of it. Just as religion was not a part of Dickens's early conception of Mrs. Clennam, so one can imagine Gradgrind without the overlay of Utilitarianism, and still see him as a significant and relevant comment on his age. Dickens's target was not a philosophy but a frame of mind, and a very nineteenth-century frame of mind. It is not often noted that much of what he says about Gradgrind and the education of his children repeats in almost identical terms what he had recently said about Grandfather Smallweed and the education of his grand-children, who "never owned a doll, never heard of Cinderella, never played at any game" and "could as soon play at leap-frog, or at cricket, as change into a cricket or a frog." It was inevitable that he should be thought at the time to be "taking on" the political economists, but he is in fact only concerned with certain of their attitudes which he regarded as symptomatic of attitudes generally current at the time. His message was little more than "we must not neglect the imagination" — a familiar one from Dickens, but an extremely timely one. (Many critics have noted that Dickens, in the upbringing of his own children, was true to his own precepts, and filled their lives with fun, games and stories. What is not so often remarked is that many of his children, when they grew up, resem-bled nothing so much as the young Gradgrinds. Several of the boys were discontented, shiftless and financially irresponsible. One of the daughters married a man she did not love to escape her father's house.)

Inevitably in a novel with such a theme mathematical and mechanical imagery plays a large part. In many superb, ironical phrases Dickens salutes mechanised, dehumanised man in his mechanised, de-na-turised environment. For example Gradgrind's house is a "calculated, cast up, balanced, and proved house," with a "lawn and garden and an infant avenue, all ruled straight like a botanical accountbook." Gradgrind's judgement of human beings and relationships, which is the core of the novel's message, is similarly mathematical, though faced with the extraor-dinary grace and vitality of a Sissy Jupe he has to admit that "there was something in this girl which could hardly be set forth in a tabular form." Gradgrind himself is a "galvanizing apparatus" and life at Stone Lodge — like life in the Clennam household, which practises a similar repression of emotion and imagination — goes "monotonously round like a piece of machinery." The "mechanical art and mystery of educating the reason" is served in his school by a master who is one of a hundred and forty "lately turned at the same time, in the same factory, on the same principles, like so many pianoforte legs." Time is the "great manufacturer" and, in a series of images in chapter 14, turns out a number of human products, varying in their satisfactoriness. In this environment, love — or rather courtship — wears a "manufacturing aspect": "love was made on these occa-sions in the form of bracelets." All is profit and loss, input and output. Mass production extends to people: "thousands upon thousands . . . aw leading the like lives," says Stephen, as usual a mouthpiece for the author, with the masters "'rating 'em as so much Power, and reg'latin 'em as if they was figures in a soom, or machines.'"

And yet fancy, rigorously excluded by the front door, pushes its way brazenly in at the back. Butt and Tillotson note the intrusion of fancy through Bounderby's assumption of low origins and Mrs. Sparsit's assumption of gentility. Even more insistent is the imagery of the novel, with its constant reference to fables, fairy tales, and the stuff of childhood and adolescent reading. Everything that was lacking in the upbringing of Louisa and Tom is present in Dickens's treatment of their story, and the Hard Fact men, who sternly outlaw fancy and emotion from their lives, become, paradoxically, the stuff of fairy-tales — mere ogres. Dickens makes the point very explicitly early on:

> Almost as soon as they could run alone, they had been made to run to the lecture-room. The first object with which they had an association, or of which they had a remembrance, was a large black board with a dry Ogre chalking ghastly white figures on it.
>
> Not that they knew, by name or nature, anything about an Ogre. Fact forbid! I only use the word to express a monster in a lecturing castle, with Heaven knows how many heads manipulated into one, taking childhood captive, and dragging it into gloomy statistical dens by the hair.
>
> (BOOK I, CHAP. 3)

And of course here and later he goes on to emphasise the imaginative deprivation of the young Gradgrinds, cut off — like the appalling young Smallweeds — from nursery rhymes, fairy tales, and the usual nourishers of childhood fancy.

But fancy has its revenge, and Coketown and its inhabitants are covered with a patina of myth and fable. Stephen, for example, betakes himself at one point to "the red brick castle of the giant Bounderby." Mrs. Sparsit, whose classical features are of the "Coriolanian style," is surrounded by Roman references drawn from the sort of story once considered suitable for schoolboy reading. She goes down to meet Mr. Harthouse "in the manner of a Roman matron going outside the city walls to treat with an invading general"; as she takes tea with Bounderby she "rather looked as if her classical countenance were invoking the infernal gods"; her position in that gentleman's household is that of "captive Princess" in attendance on his car in state-processions. Inevitably, after her drenching during the pursuit of Louisa, she is compared to a classical ruin. Not particularly fanciful herself, Mrs. Sparsit is the source of fancifulness in Dickens, and is rich in a number of other imaginative comparisons of a fabulous nature: she is a griffin, she is the "Bank Dragon keeping watch over the treasures of the mine" (though she thinks of herself as the Bank Fairy), she trails Louisa "like Robinson Crusoe in his ambuscade against the savages." Similarly Coketown, as well as being full of fairy palaces, is "red and black like the painted face of a savage." The more repulsively unimaginative the subject, the more exotic and fantastic the imagery Dickens lavishes on it, always with rich comic effect. Mr. Bounderby, for example, is a "Venus . . . risen out of the mud"; by banging his hat he becomes an oriental dancer who eventually puts her tambourine on her head. Indeed, his own description of the aspirations of the Coketown hands—"to be set up in a coach and six, and to be fed on turtle soup and venison, with a gold spoon" is drawn from the world of childish fantasy, reminding one of the young Pip's lies about Miss Havisham. Thus in all these ways Dickens drives home his message that the irrational and life-giving world of fancy cannot be suppressed, *will* be heard; as Sleary says to Gradgrind: "'You *mutht* have uth, Thquire . . . make the betht of uth; not the wurtht.'"

The fancy is not the only quality that is suppressed in Coketown and has its revenge by devious means. Religion too is perverted and slighted, yet emerges fitfully as one of the few forces that can save men from the living death which is Coketown. Dickens's religion, as it shows itself in this novel, is the same uncomplicated, unintellectual religion of good works and the heart's affections which it always had been. He is moved by the story of the Good Samaritan and the Woman Taken in Adultery more than by any Christian doctrine, however vital and central the theologians might judge it. But if he never goes beyond the "common stock of Christian phrases" which House notes as being all he has at his command, he uses it with telling force, for he sees the Political Economists as erecting a new religion, full of doctrine and empty of love. He can hardly mention the views of the "Hard Fact tribe" without tacking on an ironical religious phrase to emphasise the barrenness of their philosophy:

The M'Choakumchild school was all fact, and the school of design was all fact, and the relations between master and man were all fact, and everything was fact between the lying-in hospital and the cemetery, and what you couldn't state in

figures, or show to be purchaseable in the cheapest market
and saleable in the dearest, was not, and never should be,
world without end, Amen.

(BOOK I, CHAP. 5)

One senses in all the religious references the desperation of one who
sees the comfortable and comforting faith which he has taken for granted
all his life, and which he has believed to be the natural religion of
mankind in general, being extinguished all around and being replaced
by something brutal and materialistic. The masters in Coketown take
up a godlike stance, rule with "a sort of Divine Right," and the
Gradgrind party regale their "disciples" with "little mouldy rations of
political economy." Faith, Hope and Charity, the cornerstones of his
faith, are being ground in the "dusty little mills" of the Political
Economists; existence is becoming a "bargain across a counter" and "if
we didn't get to Heaven that way, it was not a politico-economical place,
and we had no business there." In similar vein Mr. Gradgrind, at the
moment when his daughter is about to burst in upon him to confront
him with the terrible consequences of his system, is writing in his room
what Dickens conjectures to be a study proving that the Good Samaritan
was a bad political economist. For Bitzer, that superbly mechanised
product of the system, the "whole duty of man" can be calculated as a
matter of profit and loss, and when Mr. Gradgrind becomes an M.P.,
he is described as the Member for

> ounce weights and measures, one of the representatives of the
> multiplication table, one of the deaf honourable gentlemen,
> dumb honourable gentlemen, blind honourable gentlemen,
> lame honourable gentlemen, dead honourable gentlemen, to
> every other consideration. Else wherefore live we in a Chris-
> tian land, eighteen hundred and odd years after our Master?

(BOOK I, CHAP. 14)

And if the masters deny the Christian message, or twist it to their
own ends, the Union leaders do the same. It is perhaps a sign of the
shaky balance which Dickens saw it as his mission to maintain that this
should be so. Slackbridge is a slightly more secular Chadband, and what
Dickens christens "the gospel according to Slackbridge" contains frequent references to Judas Iscariot, the serpent in the garden and the
"God-like race" of workers. Slackbridge always talks of himself in terms
of a Miltonic God punishing our first fathers: "I hurled him out from

amongst us: an object for the undying finger of scorn to point at . . . etc." It is characteristic of Dickens that Stephen should answer him with a reference to the Good Samaritan. Dickens rather frequently uses the God of the New Testament to shame the God of the Old.

For in spite of perversions and suppressions, Dickens's religion of the heart does manage to establish itself as a yardstick by which the newer, harsher creeds are measured and found wanting. Partly, of course, it makes itself felt in this novel through Stephen, and this is unfortunate. Dickens establishes, from the moment the keynote Coketown is struck, that whoever belongs to the eighteen religious denominations which had established chapels like "pious warehouses" in Coketown, "the labouring people did not." Stephen, therefore, is untypical of his class not merely in the promise he made to Rachael not to join a Union (that inexplicable promise which she didn't want him to make and apparently doesn't insist that he keep) but also in his conviction that "'the heavens is over me ahint the smoke.'" He is, as Leavis observes, a white man's nigger, and it is a measure of Dickens's lack of confidence in his power to handle the subject of the industrial worker that he has to remove Stephen so far from the average or typical before he can consider it appropriate to demand sympathy for him from the reader. The laboured allegory of his end in the "Old Hell" shaft, squeezed so dry of all emotional impact by the dreary, obvious moralising as Stephen approaches the "God of the poor," is feeble beyond belief, and one feels that it required considerable audacity on Dickens's part to write such a scene shortly after complaining about Mrs. Gaskell's characters, that he wished they would be "a little firmer on their legs." Stephen's fall down Old Hell Shaft and his long wait for hearers for his dying words amount to wanton and sadistic sentimentality. He is butchered in order to bring home to the masters and men a wholly inadequate — indeed a thoroughly false — moral.

Nevertheless, not even Stephen's blankness as a character and wrongness as a representative can totally rob his words of their force. It is wonderful how Dickens, in this brief novel, makes his moral equations almost mathematically precise but still generally manages to make them convincing. Stephen accuses his workmates of being like the Levite who ignored the man who fell among thieves ("'if I was a lyin parisht i' th' road, yo'd feel it right to pass me by, as a forrenner and stranger'") just as Mr. Gradgrind had proved to himself that the Good Samaritan was a bad economist. At the end of the book Gradgrind's appeal to Bitzer for compassion and that young machine's reply recall, but without seeming pat or unconvincing, Sissy Jupe's version of the first principle of Political Economy: "To do unto others as I would that they should do unto me." Sissy's quotation is the stuff of which Dickens's homely, kindly religion was made, as is Rachael's "'Let him who is without sin among you cast the first stone at her!'" Totally unmystical, generous, practical, tinged with sentimentality yet capable of rising to extraordinary insights. It is not always realised how closely interwoven into his thought and range of reference the Bible and its message are. It comes to his mind almost automatically when he is confronted by the brutality and materialism of his age. The philosophy of the toady Pockets, the commercial arrogance of Dombey, the greed that Merdle plays on, the stifling in children of fancy in favour of fact — the immediate response to all these is to use, or to pervert ironically, the Bible, to emphasise the shabbiness and selfishness of the proceedings. "Murdering the Innocents" is the title of the chapter which deals with Gradgrind's school.

And the third irrational force which the Philosophers fail to suppress is, of course, passion, the affections — that love which is the basis of Dickens's philosophy of life — as well as the more dangerous and destructive expressions of the sexual instinct. The whole direction of the novel is an exposition of this failure, and though this theme is dealt with less frankly and less exhaustively than the related suppression of "fancy," the crime of the attempt is clearly, in Dickens's eyes, as heavy.

In no one is the suppression completely successful. Mr. Gradgrind himself may not be conscious of any gap in his life, any dissatisfaction with the pale transparency of a wife whom he married because she was "most satisfactory as a question of figures," but he unconsciously seeks a compensation through his love for his daughter, a love which he disastrously fails to disentangle from the figures and percentages which preoccupy his conscious mind. Even Bitzer, that triumphant product of the system, on one occasion is found relieving his irrational impulses by tormenting Sissy Jupe. Though in Coketown "Nature was as strongly bricked out as killing airs and gases were bricked in," we have a sense throughout this novel of an uneasy, deceptive calm, of suppressed forces which are in danger of becoming, by that very suppression, perverted and destructive forces.

The images Dickens uses to suggest these unused powers are related to fire and water. The fires of Coketown are mirrored in the fires of Louisa's nature, where, unobserved by her father, there is "a light with nothing to rest upon, a fire with nothing to burn." In the striking scene — obviously prefiguring the similar ones in *Our Mutual Friend* involving Lizzie Hexam and Charlie—when Tom first explicitly suggests that Louisa might use her sexual hold over Bounderby to his, Tom's, advantage, she gazes into the fire, thinking her "unmanageable thoughts." When Tom leaves her after a later scene, she stands at the door gazing out over the lurid lights from the fires at Coketown and trying to establish their relationship to "her own fire within the house." All the suppressions involved in the Coketown system are related. Fire is the image she herself uses in that extraordinary and suggestive moment during the crucial interview with her father over the Bounderby proposal, he uneasily fingering his paper-knife, she gazing with a restlessness she herself only half understands over the tall chimneys of Coketown: "'There seems to be nothing there but languid and monotonous smoke. Yet when the night comes, Fire bursts out, father!'" The image is further developed when, later in the book, Dickens has to describe Louisa's resentment at Sissy Jupe's pity for her. The fire which has been suppressed is now all the more likely to rage destructively:

> A dull anger that she should be seen in her distress, and that the involuntary look she had so resented should come to this fulfilment, smouldered within her like an unwholesome fire. All closely imprisoned forces rend and destroy. The air that would be healthful to the earth, the water that would enrich it, the heat that would ripen it, tear it when caged up.
>
> (BOOK 3, CHAP. I)

The frequent use of water imagery and one powerful scene involving water have a similar purpose, but the instincts suggested by the comparison are deeper, gentler, more fruitful. In Coketown the factual and the superficial are relentlessly cultivated at the expense of the irrational, subconscious forces, but nevertheless Dickens has to suggest the depths of a nature like Louisa's, unplumbed, neglected, unaroused though they are. Of course, he only has to suggest, for there is nothing in Coketown that will ever be able to bring them to the surface:

> To be sure, the better and profounder part of her character was not within his [Harthouse's] scope of perception; for in natures, as in seas, depth answers unto depth.
>
> (BOOK 2, CHAP. 7)

For all his love and genuine desire to do right her father entirely fails to understand her nature—he has merely been "gauging fathomless deeps with his little mean excise-rod." The whole process of education for Louisa has been nothing more than "the drying up of every spring and fountain in her young heart as it gushed out." Dickens never develops the conventional image of life as a voyage — as he does in other novels — but phrases associated with such an image come naturally to his mind when he considers the waste of Louisa's life, and the perilous suppression of her best feelings. "It is the drifting icebergs setting with any current anywhere, that wreck the ships" he notes of Harthouse. In the desperate scenes with her father when she confronts him with the consequences of his system, she is described as "cast away" — for "she had suffered the wreck of her whole life upon the rock." Her descent down the staircase towards adultery is "like a weight in deep water, to the black gulf at the bottom." The powerful and suggestive scene between Tom and Harthouse, where Tom plucks to pieces rosebuds and scatters them onto the lake below is, in its level of suggestion, too subtle and complex to respond readily to analysis, but clearly it suggests among other things the wanton sacrifice not only of Louisa's virginity but also of her whole life on the altar of Tom's selfishness. In its feeling of waste and constraint the whole scene is a brilliant epitome of the book as a whole.

At this point a tribute to Dr. Leavis's account of the novel is customary, and indeed deserved, though one wonders whether the oblivion in which the novel languished before his essay is as total as is sometimes implied. And surely Shaw's essay of forty years earlier is at least as perceptive an account of the book. Do the circus scenes really bear the weight of implication which Leavis lays on them, and isn't Mr. Sleary more of a bore than he will allow — yet another, more asthmatic, mouthpiece for the author, who puts over his message more succinctly and convincingly in his own voice?

Nevertheless, though one takes Monroe Engel's point when he suggests that it is Gradgrindian to prefer *Hard Times* to the more plenteously imaginative novels of Dickens's maturity, still one cannot altogether agree with him that "curiously enough, *Hard Times* grants a scant measure of the very quality for which it argues, imaginative pleasure" (*The Maturity of Dickens*). That pleasure is there — less exuberant, less all-enveloping, less grotesque, but it is there, and it is far from scant. And there is a special fascination about a novel in which the message is so clearly matched by the manner. The fancy, the love, the compassion which Dickens brings to his picture of Coketown work subterraneously, erupt spasmodically, but they do finally and forcefully make themselves felt, win their small victories. One frequent image in the novel is that of the "short tether": Mr. Gradgrind tumbles about "within the limits of his short tether . . . annihilating the flowers of existence"; he draws a line and ties Tom down to it; he chains Louisa down to material realities. Harthouse is similarly conscious of the "stake to which he was tied." Bounderby keeps "so tight a hand" over his work people that their existence is one of unrelieved drudgery; only when he wants to entrap them is it his policy "'to give 'em line enough.'" The image arises naturally from the feeling of restriction which pervades the book, and it is probably true to say that Dickens himself was similarly restricted to a short tether—by the length of the novel, the length of each installment, the very nature of the subject matter—and chafed furiously against the limitations.

But a Dickens tethered is a very different matter from a Gradgrind tethered, for Dickens cannot help cultivating and scattering profusely those "flowers of existence" that the other annihilates. With all its faults and weaknesses, *Hard Times* does, both in its theme and the manner of its treatment, gloriously proclaim the ultimate victory of the fancy.

Gradgrind and Bounderby: Character and Caricature

Geoffrey Thurley

When, late in life, D. H. Lawrence lamented that "the middle-class cut off some of my vital vibration," he was referring to a situation Dickens knew well. "Class," Lawrence wrote, "makes a gulf across which all the best human flow is lost." All Dickens's later work is an attempt to restore this "best human flow." It is for this reason that the great tradition of the English novel moves through Dickens to Lawrence, for both men saw and felt the necessity of breaking down all the crippling barriers of pro- hibition and inhibition implicit in what Lawrence stigmatized as "the middle class *thing.*" (The phrasing is important: Lawrence makes it clear that it is not the middle class itself, a body of human beings, that is in question, but the *thing,* the consciousness of caste and barrier.)

Gradgrind's system of fact and Bounderby's business cult equally check and etiolate this best human flow. But the two men are totally dif- ferent and stand for different things. And this difference causes an im- balance never wholly set at rest in the book. Bounderby, for plot reasons, has to marry Gradgrind's daughter, Louisa; in other words, the life streams of the two men have to merge. This process merely reveals that Bounderby, the bully of humility, is caricature, and nothing but caricature. As a class-emblem (and this point is important), he is magnificent: every detail is perfect, and he remains the prototype of the self-made man, the tycoon who still exists and still plays his part in fic- tion as in life. Yet he resists integration into an emotional fabric meant

From *The Dickens Myth: Its Genesis and Structure.* © 1976 by the University of Queensland Press.

to be taken seriously. Bounderby the noisy braggart is an apt comment on the vulgar quality of life his "values" lead to. Bounderby as hurt husband is an absurdity, a fictional disaster.

Bounderby's refusal to integrate himself in the genuine emotional life of the novel only reveals what the shrewder reader had suspected: that the artistic means by which he is characterized differ widely from those used to define Gradgrind. For if Bounderby is superb social caricature, an emblem of the kind we associate with the art of Daumier, Gradgrind is a real and sympathetic human being: "The emphasis was helped by the speaker's square wall of a forehead, which had his eyebrows for its base, while his eyes found commodious cellarage in two dark caves, overshadowed by the wall. The emphasis was helped by the speaker's mouth, which was wide, thin, and hard set." The metaphor of the caves and the commodious cellarage is one of several in the book, deployed at strategic moments, which show a new trenchancy in Dickens's modes of characterization: here the figure suggests the combination of depth and stoniness eventually to bring Gradgrind to his knees. We forget neither the gloomy ring of that "cellarage," nor the vulnerability of those "commodious" depths, nor yet the suggestion of spidery movement in the brilliant use of the active verb "found" to describe the eyes. Consistently, Gradgrind holds our attention as a serious man, seriously misguided, Bounderby on the other hand is from first to last a *tour de force* of plosives—a remarkable achievement, but in a quite different literary mode.

But it was two or three novels before Dickens was to learn to keep his modes distinct, to keep characters like Bounderby clear of any emotional engagement meant to be taken seriously. The Podsnaps and Veneerings of *Our Mutual Friend* inhabit a separate plane of reality, related to the rest of the novel by their function of providing commentary on it: they remain essentially apart, in the action but not of it, hectoring and bellowing in their emblematic universe. The idea that Veneering, for example, or Boots or Brewer, should have a private life is absurd, a form of artistic suicide. At that late stage of his career, Dickens was perfectly aware that such characters belonged to a particular artistic mode, and that this mode, while of great use and adaptability, did not lend itself to involvement with other more private modes *on their terms*. This is nowhere so well revealed as in the sensitive and subtle treatment of Podsnap's daughter Georgiana, who acts as a liaison between the Podsnap-Veneering satiric mode and the mode of real relationship and individuated characterization. Georgiana's realistically conveyed dread of the eligible suitors her father throws her way acts as a commentary on her father's values, just as her father's emblematically expressed values comment on and set off the activities and purposes of people like the Lammles and Fascination Fledgeby, who are not class-caricature, but "real" people, caught up in the class-history net.

At the stage of writing *Hard Times,* Dickens had not yet acquired this sort of tact, nor the technical expertise to keep separate the different modes represented by Bounderby and Gradgrind. He was, as it were, misled, by his own initial alignment of the two men, into believing them similar characters. Thus, Gradgrind himself has to move uneasily between the modes, between satiric caricature and psychological realism. From the first description of him we are never allowed to forget the human being within the system; a little later in the first book, we are explicitly told that he "was by no means so rough a man as Mr. Bounderby. His character was not unkind, all things considered; it might have been a very kind one indeed, if he had only made some round mistake in the arithmetic that balanced it, years ago." Now in fact Dickens does not, I think, quite succeed in keeping *this* Gradgrind, the real father of Tom and Louisa, separate from "Thomas Gradgrind, Sir. A man of realities. A man of facts and calculations." His purpose, of course, demanded that the real Gradgrind should suffer because of the heartless Benthamism he has allowed to alienate him from his own deeper impulses, his children from theirs, himself from his children. The children must come to grief to demonstrate the thesis that a thorough-going Utilitarianism is destructive of the best and most real life. This is the novel's great fable, its great prophetic parable. Edmund Wilson has pointed out that Dickens's message was demonstrated with almost staggering fullness in the *Autobiography* of John Stuart Mill. Mill underwent precisely the kind of crisis experienced by Louisa Gradgrind after the botched elopement with James Harthouse. At the age of early maturity, when a young man should be emerging into the best of his intellectual and sexual life, Mill underwent a terrifying apathy, a numbness, of the kind described by Coleridge:

> A grief without a pang, void, dark, and drear,
> A stifled, drowsy, unimpassioned grief,
> Which finds no natural outlet, no relief,
> In word, or sigh, or tear—

Louisa Gradgrind, after her marriage to Bounderby, experiences "A curious passive inattention," and she turns against her only ally, Sissy

Jupe: "the stongest qualities she possessed, long turned upon themselves, became a heap of obduracy, that rose against a friend."

The treatment of Louisa and of Gradgrind himself in this chapter (the first of book 3), is impeccable. It is moreover, part of an ambitious design adumbrated in the titles Dickens gave to his three books — "Sowing," "Reaping" and "Garnering." This causal schema itself indicates that the novel was written at a transitional stage. In *Hard Times,* Dickens is moving from a fiction which, however dazzlingly expressionist in his hands, conformed to the narrative laws of realist practice, to an altogether more daring idiom, in which natural symbolism, emblem, and metaphor function as integral elements in the narrative design. I have already noted [in *The Dickens Myth*] the greater self-consciousness of the treatment of the Sleary horse-riding, which, if we contrast it with Mrs. Jarley's waxworks, appears quite consciously set up for symbolic contrast with Gradgrindery. We could extend this observation to the methods of characterization which range from penetrating realism to brilliant social caricature.

Unfortunately, however, the anomalous involvement of Bounderby in Louisa's emotional life is paralleled by certain frictions within the treatment of Gradgrind himself. For he is forced to parrot his own system in a mechanically comic way, which cuts across the realities of the superb passages in the third book in which he confesses his fundamental guilt before his daughter. As a result, it is difficult to keep the man in the mind as a consistent entity, without consciously or unconsciously excluding one or other of his aspects. Certainly, Dickens had thrown Gradgrind up into brilliantly distorted relief as the ogre of his children's nursery days: "The first object with which they had an association, or of which they had a remembrance, was a large black board with a dry Ogre chalking ghastly white figures on it." And it had already been Dickens's purpose to show the diminution of childhood ogres into normal, harmless grown-ups, as for example in the dwindling of Betsey Trotwood in *David Copperfield.* But here it is not merely childhood distortion that created the ogre. The ogre is presented to us, with Dickens's approval, in quasi-mechanistic terms:

> Indeed, as he eagerly sparkled at them from the cellarage before mentioned, he seemed a kind of cannon loaded to the muzzle with facts, and prepared to blow them clean out of the regions of childhood at one discharge. He seemed a galvanizing apparatus, too, charged with a grim mechanical substitute for the tender young imaginations that were to be stormed away.
>
> (BOOK I, CHAP. 2)

Dickens's general accuracy as a psychologist has, of course, been confirmed by behaviourism, just as the success of his comic method anticipated the gist of Bergson's account of laughter in terms of the mechanistic behaviour of the human organism. But the brilliant behaviourist organism who mouths "Facts, nothing but Facts" is not the same artistic entity as the man who has a daughter he loves, and who has to admit finally the failure of his whole life's work. So that when Gradgrind, informing Louisa of Bounderby's offer for her hand in marriage, hears her say, "'Life is very short,'" he replies — with absurd feelinglessness — according to the system: "'It is short, no doubt, my dear. Still, the average duration of human life is proved to have increased of late years. The calculations of various life assurance and annuity offices, among other figures which cannot go wrong, have established the fact.'" Even more outrageous is his response to Louisa's gentle rejoinder, "'I speak of my own life, Father.' — 'O indeed? Still,' said Mr. Gradgrind, 'I need not point out to you, Louisa, that it is governed by the laws which govern lives in the aggregate.'" Dr. Leavis finds this scene masterly in its irony; and looked at from a certain point of view perhaps it is; yet it is to me unthinkable that a man as intelligent and humane as Gradgrind should have remained so insensitive to his favourite daughter's thinly veiled reluctance, to her hurt dumb insolence in the face of Bounderby's preposterous offer. Dickens has confused his modes here: he is treating Gradgrind as the ogre of Louisa's nursery, as the "canon loaded to the muzzle with facts," after having suggested so much more.

The error is exactly inverted in the treatment of Bounderby. A magnificent and trenchant satiric figure, Bounderby is ludicrously incapable of entering into real human relations. As the bully of humility, forever harping on his mythically ghastly upbringing, Bounderby is perfectly polarized by the genteel Mrs. Sparsit, the fallen gentlewoman who acts as housekeeper-companion to him: indeed the respective hubris of the two characters — her affectation of humility suggests her ineradicable class-superiority as much as his claims to have been spawned in a ditch are meant to emphasize his greatness in getting on — keeps them perfectly equipoised. But married to Louisa, Bounderby collapses, and Dickens has to pervert the evidence to rescue his creation: Bounderby must not only bray his self-made braggartry, he must also, when occasion demands, snivel and whine. The characterization collapses at a touch and Dickens flounders so badly that the whole central book of the novel — "Reaping" — is probably the most tedious and unreal tract of its length in the whole of Dickens. The offence is compounded in the deterioration of Mrs. Sparsit — a Gorgon of the type beautifully pilloried later in *Little Dorrit* — from an efficiently kept up social Grande Dame to a more authentically Dickensian but outrageously improbable pantomime dame floundering about Lancashire in the rain, peeping through curtains and collecting evidence.

Of the two flaws — the falsification of Bounderby and the metamorphosis of Mrs. Sparsit — the second is the more interesting. For it reveals the truth that Dickens really felt bored by the lady, as indeed he was bored by the upper classes throughout his life. Mrs. Sparsit is adequately defined in terms of her "Coriolanean" nose and her stony dignity. Her collapse into a "vulgar" demonstrativeness suggests, I think, that Dickens really required more from his characters, as from people in reality, than civility and "superbness": his very failure in the depiction of the aristocracy testifies to his great love of vitality and a certain exhibitionist generosity in behaviour which he judged (I think rightly) to be eliminated by the code of the *morgue Anglaise*. Dickens was no gentleman, and we in part owe to the fact the persistence of his enormous life and fecundity.

*H*ard Times: The News
and the Novel

Joseph Butwin

Modern criticism tends to judge the novel that aims at social reform by standards that are appropriate to another kind of novel. This tendency is typified by Virginia Woolf's rejection of the novels of Arnold Bennett, H. G. Wells, and John Galsworthy according to standards that she derives from the novels of Laurence Sterne and Jane Austen:

> What odd books they are! Sometimes I wonder if we are right to call them books at all. For they leave one with so strange a feeling of incompleteness and dissatisfaction. In order to complete them it seems necessary to do something—to join a society, or, more desperately, to write a cheque. That done, the restlessness is laid, the book finished; it can be put upon the shelf, and need never be read again. But with the work of other novelists it is different. *Tristram Shandy* or *Pride and Prejudice* is complete in itself; it is self-contained; it leaves one with no desire to do anything, except indeed to read the book again, and to understand it better. . . . But the Edwardians were never interested in character in itself; or in the book in itself. They were interested in something outside. Their books, then, were incomplete as books, and required that the reader should finish them, actively and practically, for himself.

Woolf acknowledges two kinds of fiction; if we continue to judge one by the

From *Nineteenth Century Fiction* 32, no. 2 (September 1977). © 1977 by the Regents of the University of California. The University of California Press, 1977.

standards of the other, then her dissatisfaction is justified. But if we trace the novel of social reform back to its mid-Victorian practitioners, we find a literature that certainly deserves to be studied in its own terms and according to the special demands that it made on its original audience. Readers of *Hard Times* were asked to turn their attention away from the novel. Dickens's valediction in the last paragraph of the novel makes this intention clear: "Dear reader! It rests with you and me, whether, in our two fields of action, similar things shall be or not. Let them be!" He sets out to initiate "action" in a reader who is seen as something other than just a reader of novels. The novel of social reform completes itself outside the novel in a multitude of acts that may include the joining of societies and the writing of checks. It is also likely to include *further* reading as opposed to *re*reading. In the case of *Hard Times* the original readers were encouraged to see the novel as a form of journalism to be read continuously with *Household Words,* the weekly magazine in which it appeared. The novel of social reform exists in a continuum with journalism and defines its audience within the general public rather than among the community of "ideal readers" of fiction whose response justifies most literary criticism. The concept of an isolated reading public exercising no other function than the perusal of novels merely reflects the isolation of the Flaubertian artist who has become the archetype of the European novelist since Dickens.

Critical study of the novel of social reform must begin with an understanding of its differences. A great deal of the difference lies outside the novel itself within a context established by journalists, in a format congenial to journalism written for an audience that is prepared to see itself as a social force. In this essay I will re-create the journalistic milieu of *Hard Times,* which I take to epitomize the novel of social reform in England. (I call *Hard Times* a novel of social reform rather than the more familiar *"roman social"* used by Louis Cazamian in *Le Roman social en Angleterre [1830–1850] [Paris: H. Didier, 1904],* because most novels are "social" insofar as most novels describe and even analyze social conditions without necessarily encouraging any form of political action. Charles Kingsley, Elizabeth Gaskell, and Dickens are reformers.) This does not mean that the problems of the novel can be explained away by an outside appeal. On the contrary, *Hard Times* presents certain critical problems which stem precisely from Dickens's understanding of his genre and which I will try to explain in terms appropriate to the genre.

Hard Times was first read by a public which tended to take its newspapers more seriously than its novels. Abundant testimony in the

1850s locates a new source of power in public opinion, and over and over opinion is linked with the press. When novelists set out to enlist public opinion on social issues they generally understood that they were following the lead of the journalists. In an early venture of this kind Dickens follows Oliver Twist into the Magistrate's Court and shifts into the present tense that he reserves for the observation of continuous social abuse in that novel:

> Although the presiding Genii in such an office as this, exercise a summary and arbitrary power over the liberties, the good name, the character, almost the lives, of Her Majesty's subjects, especially of the poorer class; and although, within such walls enough fantastic tricks are daily played to make the angels blind with weeping; they are closed to the public, save through the medium of the daily press.

Critical reception of novels more strictly given over to social issues in the 1840s indicates that they were being read as something other than novels. The *Edinburgh Review* justified W. R. Greg's long (and largely unfavorable) review of Elizabeth Gaskell's *Mary Barton* with the running head: "*Not to be regarded as a mere Novel.*" Similarly the *Manchester Guardian* (February 28, 1849) indentified the book as a form of current history or journalism masquerading as a novel: "There are popular works published in the form of novels that depict either important historical events of bygone years, or the passing realities of the present, in such an intense manner that the impression conveyed is stamped more vividly and indelibly on the mind . . . than from the study of history properly so-called." This, of course, is just what the novelists of social reform intended. Greg and the *Guardian* reviewer were protecting the domain of journalism. Both criticized the novel for errors in fact and analysis. The novelists themselves understood that they were entering that domain and in some cases improving upon it. Charles Kingsley praised *Mary Barton* "for the awful facts contained in it." He saw that there are certain functions served by novelistic "facts" that may even surpass the instructive powers of the press. "In spite of blue-books and commissions, in spite of newspaper horrors and parliamentary speeches, Manchester riots and the 10th of April, the mass of higher orders cannot yet be aware of what a workman's home is like in the manufacturing districts." Again, his eye is on facts and their impact on public opinion which he locates among "the higher orders." The interest of this kind of criticism then turns to the distribution of the novel and consequent action on the part of the readership, neither of which has anything to do with the criteria described by Virginia Woolf in her essay on the Edwardians. The reviewer in this case is also a preacher and a publicist and a novelist of social reform. He begins his review of *Mary Barton* with a call to action: "Had we wit and wisdom enough, we would placard its sheets on every wall, and have them read aloud from every pulpit, till a nation, calling itself Christian, began to act upon the awful facts contained in it, not in the present peddling and desultory manner, but with an united energy of shame and repentance proportionate to the hugeness of the evil." Kingsley's own novel, *Yeast,* had just concluded its six-month run in *Fraser's* where the review of *Mary Barton* appeared. By this time the periodical press had become the ideal vehicle for the news and the novel.

Ever since the success of *Pickwick* had allowed Dickens to leave the *Morning Chronicle* in 1836, it had been his ambition to unite the functions of the newspaper and the novel. *Bentley's Miscellany, Master Humphrey's Clock,* and the *Daily News* all failed to satisfy that impulse before 1850 when all of his ideas jelled around a journal of social reform. His earliest intentions for *Household Words* included the idea that it should provide the proper context for novels like *Mary Barton.* Immediately he wrote Gaskell: "There is no living English writer whose aid I would desire to enlist in preference to the authoress of Mary Barton (a book that most profoundly affected and impressed me) . . . all will seem to express the general mind and purpose of the journal, which is the raising up of those that are down, and the general improvement of our social condition."

Dickens's public declaration in the "Preliminary Word" to the first number of *Household Words* (March 30, 1850) would appear at a glance to have a quite different aim in mind. He celebrates "Fancy" and the "imagination" and promises to reveal the "thousand and one tales" too often obscured by the smoke of the factories and their flaming chimneys. One might ask how the Condition of England is to be improved by the telling of tales. Through the agency of fancy and the imagination a whole class may be able to adopt the experience of another class. In order for the facts of industrial life to take hold they must be bodied forth in a fanciful way. Then something akin to Romantic sympathy may be made to prick the conscience of a class. But this activation of middle-class sympathy is not to be confused with "class consciousness" on the part of the beneficiaries of that sympathy. Dickens knows that this mixture of fact and fancy could become extremely volatile. At the end of his introduction he moves without apparent transition into a denial of revolutionary intention:

Some tillers of the field into which we now come, have been before us, and some are here whose high usefulness we readily acknowledge, and whose company it is an honour to join. But, there are others here — Bastards of the Mountain, draggled fringe on the Red Cap, Panders to the basest passions of the lowest natures — whose existence is a national reproach. And these, we should consider it our highest service to displace.

The Dickensian impression of the "Red Cap" and the "Mountain" had recently been kindled by events in France. The radical press in England self-consciously followed the French example. Julian Harney called himself "L'ami du peuple" in the *Red Republican,* a weekly journal published from June 1850 to July 1851, and Dickens makes it clear from the start that he is no Harney, certainly no Marat, and that his audience are not *sans-culottes.*

A journal dedicated to "the raising up of those that are down" finds its ideal audience among those who are not down. Dickens's other contribution to the first number of *Household Words* begins with the favorite formula of the middle-class reformer: "As one half of the world is said not to know how the other half lives, so it may be affirmed that the upper half of the world neither knows nor greatly cares how the lower half amuses itself." The article, called "The Amusements of the People," affirms for the lower orders that right that Sleary claims for all people in *Hard Times:* "We believe that these people have a right to be amused." Amusement — in this case vaudeville theater — is also education. For the education of the poor Dickens rejects the "Polytechnic Institution in Regent Street" in favor of the theater because "there is a range of imagination in most of us, which no amount of steam-engines will satisfy." The "amusements" and the instruction of the poor are not served by print. Joe Whelks, as Dickens calls the man of the people, "is not much of a reader, has no great store of books, no very commodious room to read in, no very decided inclination to read, and no power at all of presenting vividly before his mind's eye what he reads about." In other words, he is telling his audience, if you are reading this article you are not a part of "the other half." His audience is thus identified as a reading public to whose amusement and instruction is added the responsibility of reform.

Dickens initiated *Household Words* in 1850 with many of the ideas that would animate the writing of *Hard Times* four years later. The novel represents the principles of the journal as they are stated in its first issue—its belief in the redemptive power of fancy, especially in the industrial milieu, its defense of popular amusement, and its warning not to confuse middle-class reform with demagoguery.

Six months after the conclusion of *Hard Times,* as an introduction to the eleventh volume of *Household Words,* Dickens restates the principles of his journal in a leading article called "That Other Public" (February 3, 1855). The threats of the "Red Cap" have receded and been replaced by the corruption of successful politicians and entrepreneurs. The machinations of both tend to render the public sluggish and recalcitrant on issues of reform. The means of both are essentially the same: they manipulate the press through the contrivance of favorable publicity. During the busy first week of February 1855 when Palmerston was to become Prime Minister, several papers reported that he had hired a few disreputable journalists to convince the American press of his pacific international policy. Without naming names Dickens condemns a politician who would "purchase remote puffery among the most puff-ridden people ever propagated on the face of the earth." Since the time of his visit to the United States in 1841, the American example would bring to Dickens's mind the worst excesses of the press and of the promoters who habitually misuse it. From Palmerston he turns to the unnamed author "of a little book of Memoirs" lately published. The list of impostures shows the subject to be P. T. Barnum:

> Does the "smart" Showman, who makes such a Mermaid, and makes such a Washington's Nurse, and makes such a Dwarf, and makes such a Singing Angel upon earth, and makes such a fortune, and, above all, makes such a book— does *he* address the free and enlightened Public of the great United States: the Public State of Schools, Liberal Tickets, First-chop Intelligence, and Universal Education? No, no. That other Public is the sharks'-prey.

In many ways Barnum's Dwarf and Angel—Tom Thumb and Jenny Lind—fulfill the needs that Dickens describes in his articles on "The Amusements of the People" and in *Hard Times.* A nation governed by Gradgrinds would seem to need its Barnums. Unfortunately, Barnum asks too high a price. All of his tricks, pranks, and promotions represent the utter perversion of the art that Dickens was cultivating in *Household Words.* Dickens's fictions become Barnum's lies; the public's willingness to absorb fantasy becomes downright credulity. Barnum represents the self-serving publicist whose aim is not to inform but to advertise. In his autobiography Barnum describes the way the press serves the purposes of the entrepreneur:

> Whatever your occupation or calling may be, if it needs support from the public, *advertise* it thoroughly and efficiently, in some shape or other, that will arrest public attention. . . . In this country [the United States], where everybody reads the newspapers, the man must have a thick skull who does not see that these are the cheapest and best mediums through which he can speak to the public, where he is to find his customers. Put on the *appearance* of business, and generally the *reality* will follow.

Household Words included no commercial advertisement beyond the announcement of its own future publication, the continuation of a serial or the appearance of separate volumes. When a distributor slipped a sheet of advertisement into one of the issues and angry readers complained to the *Times,* Dickens traced the "disgraceful effusion" to its source and reported his findings in a letter to the editor (*Times,* July 10 and 20, 1852). Dickens shared Carlyle's disdain for the new art of advertisement with its seven-foot hats and quack medicines.

The kind of advertisement practiced by Barnum taps what Dickens recognized as a basic human need, the need to be amused. By the time he undertook the editorship of *Household Words* Dickens had begun to interpret the old injunction to amuse *and* instruct as a mandate for social reform that could be best fulfilled through the medium of journalism. Much of what he writes in *Household Words* amounts to the definition and education of a good, responsive, and politically responsible public that would counter the false appeal of the Barnum breed and establish a firm constituency for the Dickensian enterprise. In *Hard Times* Dickens seeks a public that has been trained to respond to journalism. Various stylistic devices encourage readers to verify and test the fiction outside the novel. When the novel is made to stand alone, its weakness lies in an editorial policy that defers specific issues out of the mouths of novelistic characters and into the journalistic setting where the middle-class public is encouraged to turn from spurious demagogues and entrepreneurial boosters to the reliable guidance of the journalist.

The installments of *Hard Times* are the only signed articles in *Household Words.* The name "Charles Dickens" appears above each one, and readers are invited to take the novel as the editor's own comment on the

"times." Each installment seems to enjoy both the status of a leading article and the special identity of a signed novel inserted into the journal.
The reader who meets the novel in the journal comes away with a quite
different impression of the meaning of the fiction than the reader of the
hard-cover volume called *Hard Times for These Times.* In *Household Words*
it is simply *Hard Times.* The reader of the journal did not need the ex-
panded title. Every article appeared under the sign of novelty; all was
news, all was timely. Having read the installment, the reader continues
into other reports, equally timely. Regular readers of *Household Words*
might recall an article on the Manchester library, "Manchester Men at
Their Books" (December 17, 1853), when in the April 22, 1854 issue
they read in *Hard Times* about a library in Coketown; other articles
about the London poor or the Preston strike are likely to linger in the
mind of the reader of the novel. It is not so much that the reader will
transfer knowledge directly from one sphere to another, from fact to fiction and back again, as that he reads with the inclination to do so. Other
novels that invoke the facts of historical or contemporary life do not
necessarily encourage verification. *Hard Times,* by virtue of its format,
does. The fiction leads the reader to the threshold of fact; the threshold is
easily crossed within the same journal. The inquisitive reader will go
further. Within the text of the novel Dickens encourages these excur-
sions outside the novel. He teases the reader with fictions that retain the
latent authority of fact.

The facts of industrial life are bound to represent opinions, and it is
Dickens's reluctance to lodge fully developed opinions within the text
that renders *Hard Times* incomplete as a novel of social reform. As we
shall see, in one significant deletion he takes words out of the mouth of a
character, Stephen Blackpool, and lets them live in a series of reports on
factory safety that appeared before and after the run of the novel. The
reformer who characterizes his enemies as revolutionaries — "Bastards of
the Mountain" — cannot let his hero wear a red cap. Deletions and swift
allusions sent the reader back into the journal and locate the source of
social improvement as middle-class opinion guided by a responsible
reformer-journalist. The reader is led out of the novel into the journal.
This process begins with the substitution of fact for fiction.

Hard Times is generally read as a denigration of "hard facts" but at
the same time it may be seen as Dickens's attempt to renew rather than
reduce the status of fact. He sets out to reclaim fact from the hands of the
statisticians by showing that much of what passes for fact in Coketown is
really fiction. A master says "that he would 'sooner pitch his property into the Atlantic'" if he is "not left entirely alone" to do as he pleases with

his own. "Another prevalent fiction," says Dickens. Any worker who saves his money can become a master or at least a rich man. "This, again, was among the fictions of Coketown." The by-play of "fact" and "fiction" is especially evident when the novel is read in the journal. An article in *Household Words* calls the image of marital bliss that hides the legal inequality of man and woman "One of our Legal Fictions" (April 29, 1854). On the last page of the article a discreet advertisement announces the appearance of "the SIXTH PORTION of a New Work of Fiction called *Hard Times.*" Fiction is a pejorative word only in a world self-consciously governed by fact. Dickens writes in both worlds.

Both as a novelist and a journalist Dickens contrives fictional proper nouns as a masquerade of fact. Outside the novel Dickens resisted any attempts to identify "Coketown." Literal identification would "localize" and therefore narrow the application of the story. But within the text he invites his readers to ask whether or not a real town exists behind the pseudonym: "Stone Lodge was situated on a moor within a mile or two of a great town — called Coketown in the present faithful guide-book." "A mile or two from Coketown" or even "a mile or two from a great town called Coketown" is a defensible fiction. Knowledge of English geography would reveal no Coketown. But phrased as it is, the town invites indentification, especially when we remind ourselves that for its first readers the "present faithful guide-book" was *Household Words,* a journal filled with factual description of conditions in real factory towns. The reader is always on the edge of the fact in the installments of *Hard Times.* At any point the author might break through as he does in "One of Our Legal Fictions" to say "this is a true story." Charlotte and Robert Desborough (in that article) could be identified. The emergent meaning of the fiction is always validated by the constant possibility of fact. The journalist stands behind the novelist, and the power of the press is brought to bear on a novel whose purpose is "the general inprovement of our social condition."

The literal identification of Oldham or Preston or Wigan would mean nothing. Dickens frequently makes his point by making up names. Coketown is more descriptive and evocative than Preston. In "On Strike," which we take to be a factual, journalistic report of a trip to Preston, Dickens meets a nasty (but convenient) antagonist "whom I had already began [sic] to call in my own mind Mr. Snapper, and whom I may as well call by that name here as by any other." Snapper is a straw man; he serves a purpose but he is not a real, historical person. A reader accustomed to modern "objective" journalism is less prepared to accept Dickens's identification of an obnoxious potential demagogue as "Gruffshaw" when other, reliable reports reveal only a "Grimshaw" among the leaders of the strike. Gruff is a nice replacement for grim. A reader might recognize the hand of the novelist in this anonymous report. A few months earlier, in another article about Preston, a well-known leader of the workers named Cowell is misidentified as Cowler. In this case the change of name is meaningless and a little careless. The author was James Lowe, a journalist who knew Preston well. Lowe corrected himself six years later in his report to the Social Science Association where he names both Cowell and Grimshaw. When we look back to 1853 and 1854, I think that we can safely say that Lowe just made a mistake, but that Dickens deliberately mixed newsmaking and novel writing in order to gain the best of both in *Household Words*.

Together the techniques of the novelist and the journalist can be made to serve the rhetorical function of persuasion. And yet in a novel that is so harsh on other forms of rhetoric — Slackbridge's oratory, Bounderby's self-aggrandizement, and Sleary's advertisement — Dickens is unable to create a worthy spokesman for the poor. Stephen Blackpool, for one, is almost mute. Thanks to a significant deletion from an early speech, Stephen is barely allowed to give specific designation to the complaint of the factory workers, and thanks to the same deletion we never know why it is that he is unable to join the union. His public declaration leaves questions unanswered: "But I ha' my reasons — mine, yo see — for being hindered; not on'y now, but awlus — awlus — life long!" As it happens, he has made a vow to Rachael, but that vow is hidden in the deleted passage. In chapter 13 Stephen is sitting a night watch over his drunken wife. He very nearly allows her to poison herself with an unprescribed dose of medicine when Rachael wakes up and takes the matter in hand. In the dialogue that follows she alludes to a dead sister whose death is explained by Stephen in a passage that made it through the manuscript into the corrected proofs before it was cancelled:

> "Thou'st spoken o' thy little sister. There agen! Wi' her child arm tore off afore thy face." She turned her head aside, and put her hand [up]. "Where dost thou ever hear or read o' us — the like o' us — as being otherwise than onreasonable and cause o' trouble? Yet think o' that. Government gentlemen come and make's report. Fend of the dangerous machinery, box it off, save life and limb; don't rend and tear human creeturs to bits in a Chris'en country! What follers? Owners sets up their throats, cries out, 'Onreasonable! Inconvenient! Troublesome!' Gets to Secretaries o' States wi' deputations, and

nothing's done. When do we get there wi' our deputations,
God help us! We are too much int'rested and nat'rally too far
wrong t'have a right judgment. Haply we are; but what are
they then? I' th' name o' th' muddle in which we are born and
live and die, what are they then?" "Let such things be,
Stephen. They only lead to hurt, let them be!" "I will, since
thou tell'st me so. I will. I pass my promise."

Why delete? Dickens was certainly pressed throughout the writing of
Hard Times to cut it down to fit twenty short installments, but it is hard to
believe that a passage of such brevity and such importance had to be
sacrificed for space. It may be that at the last moment he decided that
this was simply bad drama, that Rachael's arbitrary prohibition was
weaker than Stephen's unexplained mystery.

Let us say that Dickens rids himself of one dramatic gaffe; he also
avoids a subtle connection with the rest of the novel and a major statement of a specific industrial complaint coming from a factory worker. At
the end of the last chapter four paragraphs describe the future of the sur-
vivors. Each ends with a similar refrain: "Such a thing was to be. . . .
Such things were to be. . . . Such a thing was never to be. . . . These
things were to be." Only the last of these confirms a cheerful future that
is dependent on "no fantastic vow, or bond . . . or pledge" but on Sissy's
dutiful promotion of "childish lore . . . imaginative graces and delights"
among her children. It is then that Dickens in the final paragraph enjoins the reader to promote "similar things. . . . Let them be!" Taken as
an affirmation of responsible action, this last "Let them be" is a repudiation of the cynical carelessness of the Harthouse philosophy, "What will
be, will be," which is another way of saying "laissez-faire." Stephen calls
this policy on the part of the manufacturers "lettin alone." The final allusion to vows and pledges seems to imply a freedom from the
unreasonable constraint by which Stephen was bound doubly in promises to Rachael and to his wife. The last "Let them be" is an ironic
reflection on Rachael's opposite use of the phrase. In the deleted passage
she had said, "Let such things be, Stephen" in a way that means "Let
them alone. Desist." The final "Let them be" means "Let them exist. Act
in such a way that these lessons will prevail." It is an injunction to action
on the part of his readership. Now it may be that Dickens foresaw a problem and was unwilling to allow any ironic reflection on Stephen's promise to Rachael. The uncorrected version could be taken to mean that
workers are wrong to "let such things be" in Rachael's sense. When one

considers the truth (and simple eloquence) of Stephen's complaint in the deleted passage along with his pathetic fate, the vow that he makes to Rachael can be made to look at least as unfortunate as his marriage vow—to evoke shades of the red cap and the mountain and a kind of working-class activism that Dickens truly means to avoid. If there is to be any political initiative, it is to be taken not by the working class but by the reading class to whom he safely returns responsibility in the last paragraph of the book.

Stephen's complaint on the subject of preventable accidents is not entirely lost to the novel. It is deferred to a highly elliptical passage in his last speech, spoken as he lies dying beside the Old Hell Shaft. Of course, Stephen's physical condition at this point does not allow a developed argument. Stephen reminds Rachael that the Old Hell Shaft has caused many deaths and been the subject of many petitions from the miners unheeded in Parliament. "When it were in work, it killed wi'out need; when 'tis let alone, it kills wi'out need." Stephen's death becomes another industrial accident. Now, to complete his argument, Rachael's little sister is resurrected in a brief allusion which is not likely to have much resonance in a novel in which she has only been mentioned once, two hundred pages or two months earlier not (thanks to the deletion) as an industrial victim but simply as a dead child among the angels. Now her death is explained not as a result of brutal amputation but as a result of "sickly air":

> "Thy little sister, Rachael, thou hast not forgot her. . . . Thou know'st . . . how thou didst work for her, seet'n all day long in her little chair at thy winder, and how she died, young and misshapen, awlung o' sickly air as had'n no need to be, an' awlung o' working people's miserable homes. A muddle! Aw a muddle!"

The reader jumps from the immediate situation into the question of preventable accidents in the mines and the unwillingness of legislators to act. From there we follow the weak link of Rachael's forgotten sister into conditions in the factories and the cities which, presumably, might also be amended by legislation and enforcement. A reader who has only the novel in hand may well be perplexed.

This digression does not seem to serve the immediate demands of the story of Stephen's attempt to clear himself of guilt or to say a few last words to the woman he loves. As a political prescription this mingling of open pits and petitions, a misshapen sister and miserable homes is somehow incomplete, no more than a "muddle." Dickens certainly does not wish to limit his comment here to a suggestion that unused mine shafts should be fenced off. A reader familiar with contemporary controversy would have heard the description of a man whose life has been "mangled . . . out of him" in an unfenced "shaft" as an allusion to the factory as well as the mine.

The Factory Act of 1844 required the fencing of open shafts that housed dangerous machinery, but inspection had always been inadequate and the owners unwilling to sacrifice the expense necessary for safety. In 1854 and 1855 the inspectors, with support from the Home Secretary and an informed public, began to enforce regulation. As we shall see, articles in *Household Words* contributed to the making of a public policy that would draw the masters out into the open.

The ellipses in Stephen's argument in *Hard Times* can be filled in by further reading in *Household Words*. In the number that included the fourth installment of the novel, an article by Henry Morley called "Ground in the Mill" also appeared (April 22, 1854). The article is really an extended statement of the complaint that Dickens would delete from Stephen's speech three weeks later. Within that passage Dickens had inserted a footnote directing the reader back to "Ground in the Mill." Footnotes frequently refer to other articles in *Household Words*. In this case the note was deleted with the passage, and the modern editor assumes that it was done because an "intrusion of this kind of documentation would distract his readers from the realities of his fictional world." As editor of *Household Words* Dickens himself was not intent on maintaining the inviolability of his fictional world. Different political intention rather than the different status of fact and fiction may have prompted Dickens to reduce the association between the opinions of fictional characters and the editorial stance of *Household Words*. Within the novel specific complaints of the workers are abbreviated, and attention is diverted from the novel to the journal where the editorial voice suggests action on the part of the middle class rather than the working class. An eloquent Stephen would be as unreliable as Slackbridge. Neither Morley nor Dickens advises initiative on the part of the workers; both hold the owners responsible, but neither expects much response from the owners without coercion. The owners speak directly to the Home Secretary through their "deputations." Their victims have no voice but that of their middle-class sympathizers whose effective power resides in public opinion.

In 1854 the reading public was prepared to consider conditions in the factories. The strikers at Preston were just about to give up their long and well-publicized struggle when *Hard Times* began to appear in the April issue of *Household Words*. Soon news from Crimea would seem to drive the Condition of England into oblivion, but journalists remained "to show the evils of that carelessness, which, in great matters and little matters, from Balaklava to the Lancashire coal-pits, is undoubtedly becoming a rather remarkable feature of our national character." If we take the monthly reviews and daily press to be both a gauge and a guide of public opinion, we may measure the relative impact of the novel of social reform and the journal in which it was placed. As we might guess, since Dickens allowed the journal to absorb the most pressing issues related to the industrial theme, it was the journal and not the novel that made itself felt in the press and on the platforms of public debate.

By the mid-1850s a press that was generally hostile to the claims of labor was ready to acknowledge as wholesome the appeal that the new, national unions were making to the court of public opinion. "It is public opinion, and that only which can assist the workmen in the recovery of their 'rights' if any such have been lost. From this all-controlling force manufacturers are no more exempt than any other classes in the kingdom" (*Times,* January 2, 1852). But until the renewal of the debate of the factory acts in 1854 the manufacturers were not inclined to consult public opinion. Strikes could be suppressed quietly, and the strikers' claim to higher wages could never wholly penetrate a community still dominated by the laws of a free and open market. It was the high incidence of preventable accidents in the factories that would fix the attention of middle-class reformers and finally draw the masters into the public arena. Here economic arguments meant less, and the humanitarian argument could hold its own. And in this case legislation and enforcement could be retained as a middle-class enterprise without the necessity of intervention from the beneficiaries. (It was not until 1882 that a working man, J. D. Prior of the Amalgamated Carpenters, was made an Inspector.) Factory safety, the latent basis of Stephen Blackpool's complaint in *Hard Times,* would become the favored crusade of Dickens and Morley in *Household Words.*

All of the emotional appeal of Rachael's little sister "wi' her child arm tore off afore thy face" is released in the first of Morley's articles. He begins the argument of "Ground in the Mill" with little vignettes of children who are caught in moments of play and punished by the machines:

"Watch me do a trick!" cried such a youth to his fellow, and put his arm familiarly within the arm of the great ironhearted chief. "*I'll* show you a trick," gnashed the pitiless monster. A coil of strap fastened his arm to the shaft, and round he went. His leg was cut off, and fell into the room, his arm was broken in three or four places, his ankle was broken, his head was battered; he was not released alive.

Another is "caught as he stood on a stool wickedly looking out of window at the sunlight and the flying clouds." Imprisoned children punished, a taste for freedom and play quelled. No question of circuses here, and, for that matter, no question of polytechnic education. In conclusion Morley describes a factory school (also provided by the Act of 1844) which is flawed by complete carelessness and irregularity rather than by the rigors of the school room in *Hard Times.* The novel describes the price paid by children of the middle class rather than the working class. Rachael's sister is the only factory child mentioned in *Hard Times.* "Ground in the Mill" is dense with examples, and all are true. Twenty-six examples of death and mutilation have almost no statistical force, but they argue strongly when described one by one. Dickens and his writers replace one kind of fact with another, and as journalists they are unrelenting. One can follow the fate of their agitation in the press and what one finds is a public that reads, responds, reacts in decidedly nonliterary ways. This then was the public for the novel as well.

In an article called "Fencing With Humanity," written a year after "Ground in the Mill," Morley describes the campaign mounted by the manufacturers since that time. The Home Secretary has ordered enforcement and "instantly a large number of millowners fly to the platform, deliver and hear angry orations, form deputations, and declare themselves a slaughtered interest." This is Stephen's deleted speech cleansed of dialect: "What follers? Owners sets up their throats, cries out, 'Onreasonable! Inconvenient! Troublesome!' Gets to Secretaries o' States wi' deputations." The novel moves toward a statement that is made in the journal. Together they seek the same public, and in this case the effect can be measured by the response of competitive publicists. "Fencing With Humanity" is dated April 14, 1855, a Saturday. It appeared for sale on the preceding Wednesday (April 11). On the following Tuesday (April 17) a meeting of manufacturers calling themselves The National Association for the Amendment of the Factory Law met in Manchester. They would enlist public opinion which, they recognized, had recently turned against them. *Household Words* was selected by the chairman as an example of the most obvious opposition.

The chairman was the ubiquitous W. R. Greg, and the meeting was given thorough coverage in the next day's *Guardian*. According to Greg, the current troubles of the manufacturers are a result of "the amount of ignorance and prejudice and ill-will towards them on the part of the community-at-large." He produces an example of this ill-will:

> Dickens's "Household Words" — (hear, hear) — a paragraph from which he would read to them, and which had been very good-naturedly put into the London morning papers only a few days ago. He would read it not merely to give an idea, if proof were necessary, of the ignorance and prejudice existing against them, but because in it were stated facts, partial facts, but still facts, on which were grounded, no doubt, the general feeling against the millowners which pervaded the community, and the abuse which was then lavished upon them as a body. — (hear, hear). (*Manchester Guardian,* April 18, 1855)

After reading an especially unflattering paragraph from Morley's article of the preceding week, Greg launches into his own statistics. The government, he says, finds time to prosecute factory owners for the death of one worker in seventy thousand when thanks to its own neglect men are dying in Crimea at the rate of one thousand per week. And more in that vein. Greg is seconded by a Mr. Turner who knows the value of these awesome numbers in the making of public opinion. He only hopes that the chairman's words will "travel throughout the length and breadth of the land, and prove an antidote to the trash, the poison, published on Saturday in 'Household Words.'" He attacks "philanthropic writers": "They wished, of course, not only to write works which might create a popularity for themselves, but the publishers of twopenny publications wished to add grist to their mill — and so the one wrote and the other published for the prejudices of the people." Dickens is accused of barnumizing. After receiving support from a speaker with the charmingly Dickensian name of Holdforth, Turner enjoins his fellows to "charge the enemy, and they would soon beat down his ranks."

Four weeks after the meeting in Manchester, Morley responded to the assault on "twopenny publications [written] for the benefit of pseudo-philanthropists." The response, titled "Death's Cyphering-Book," is a fairly faithful record of the transactions at Manchester accompanied by a commentary that clearly bears the mark of Dickens's own repugnance for "arithmatical" calculation of life and death. Greg's statistics were supposed to reduce the threat of unfenced machinery. Through a series of imaginative counter examples Morley reduces to absurdity "the assumption that arithmetic will ever work out questions of moral right and wrong." By such calculation a man who spends only five minutes out of a long lifetime as a murderer cannot be found guilty, especially when he could have had so many more victims. "Our pseudo-philanthropic readers" are left to decide the question.

However they are labeled, these readers are Dickens's intended audience, a morally responsive middle class whose collective power is embodied in public opinion. In one of his few vocal outbursts, Stephen Blackpool is allowed to aim his attack not at bad working conditions but at bad publicity. Stephen complains to Bounderby:

> "Look how you considers of us, an writes of us, an talks of us, and goes up wi' yor deputations to Secretaries o' State 'bout us, and how yo are awlus right, and how we are awlus wrong, and never had'n no reason in us sin ever we were born."

If Stephen cannot speak for himself — and Dickens says that he cannot — others will. Stephen's speech to Bounderby invites the appearance of a spokesman who never appears in the novel. Whatever was to be said in his behalf as a specific complaint that might require specific reform would be said in the editorial columns of the journal.

When *Hard Times* was published as an independent volume immediately after its conclusion in *Household Words,* it was bound to appear incomplete, even to those readers who came to it with the correct expectation of a novel that would answer pressing social questions. Reviewers in both *Blackwood's* and the *Westminster Review* declared that the public was cheated out of a timely statement on the industrial theme. "The name of the book and the period of its publication alike deluded the public. We anticipated a story . . . of the unfortunate relationship between masters and men which produced the strike of Preston; and this most legitimate subject, at once for public inquiry and for the conciliating and healing hand of genius, to whom both belligerents were brothers, might have well employed the highest powers." Both reviewers are perplexed by the turn to the educational theme which strikes them as fanciful and irrelevant.

Dickens, if he had wished to, could have justified himself by pointing to *Household Words.* Another novelist of social reform would be less inclined to let the reader wander beyond the text. In *North and South,* which began in serial form (September 2, 1854) a month after the completion of *Hard Times,* Elizabeth Gaskell reopens the industrial theme with a fully articulate working man, Nicholas Higgins, who reads books and responds to them, who explains the rationale of the strike and who understands the value of "public opinion" and knows how it is to be won. Higgins meets a master, John Thornton, who is stubborn but intelligent and eventually willing to change. Before the novel is over, Higgins and Thornton have begun to reconcile their differences and have embarked on a cooperative enterprise. It may be that *North and South* is too pat, too perfect. In this case Gaskell is less willing than Dickens to recognize that the novel of social reform takes a modest position in the literary and political processes of a world that refuses to perfect itself.

Muddle and Wonderful No-Meaning: Verbal Irresponsibility and Verbal Failures in *Hard Times*

Peter Bracher

As he lies helpless and fatally injured at the bottom of Old Hell Shaft, Stephen Blackpool, the victimized mill hand of Charles Dickens's *Hard Times,* has been able to look up the shaft to a patch of sky. Through the nights he has watched a solitary star. Speaking to Rachael of his ordeal, he says:

> It ha' shined upon me . . . in my pain and trouble down below. It ha' shined into my mind. I ha' look'n at 't and thowt o' thee, Rachael, till the muddle in my mind have cleared awa, above a bit, I hope. If soom ha' been wantin' in un-nerstan'in me better, I, too, ha' been wantin' in unnerstan'in them better. When I got thy letter, I easily believen that what the yoong ledy sen and done to me, and what her brother sen and done to me, was one, and that there were a wicked plot betwixt 'em. When I fell, I were in anger wi' her, an' hurryin on t' be as onjust t' her as oothers was t' me. But in our judgments, like as in our doins, we mun bear and forbear. In my pain an' trouble, lookin up yonder, — wi' it shinin on me — I ha' seen more clear, and ha' made it my dyin prayer that aw th' world may on'y coom toogether more, an' get a better unnerstan'in o' one another, than when I were in 't my own weak seln.
>
> (BOOK 3, CHAP. 6)

From *Studies in the Novel* 10, no. 3 (Fall 1978). © 1978 by North Texas State University.

In what are almost his final words, Stephen touches on several of the important themes in the novel. One is to repeat his view that life is a "muddle." From our first encounter with him, Stephen has with refrainlike regularity described his personal situation and life itself as "awlus a muddle." In this his last important speech in the novel, however, Stephen provides a significant clarification of his view: he links muddle to failures in understanding — the "muddle in my mind" — and tells Rachael that as a result of his ordeal he has been able to see more clearly than before. And so he dies hoping that people can come together through better understanding, suggesting that this may be a way to clear up the muddle. Stephen's speech singles out human failures in communication and blames them for the muddle of life. This is an important idea in the development of *Hard Times*.

While it would be a mistake to say that in presenting this idea Stephen articulates the central theme of the novel, certainly lack of understanding and breakdowns in communication are intimately linked with the muddle depicted in the book and the misfortunes consequent upon it. Dickens masterfully and sometimes savagely exposes verbal muddle and exhibits assorted abuses of language so that *Hard Times* presents a verbal jungle in which "a better unnerstan'in o' one another" is all but impossible. In very important ways his story is about failures of communication. They become an integral part of the pattern of failures that Dickens exposes and indicts in the novel, and hence they assume major thematic significance.

From our first encounter with it in the Gradgrind school, the world of *Hard Times* displays a strong streak of surrealistic absurdity. One of the most startling passages in the famous opening chapters of the book presents a government inspector of schools expounding an extraordinary philosophy of interior decoration:

> "Now, let me ask you girls and boys, Would you paper a room with representations of horses?"
>
> After a pause, one half of the children cried in chorus, "Yes, Sir!" Upon which the other half, seeing in the gentleman's face that Yes was wrong, cried out in chorus, "No, Sir!" — as the custom is, in these examinations.
>
> "Of course, No. Why wouldn't you?"
>
> A pause. One corpulent slow boy, with a wheezy manner of breathing, ventured the answer, Because he wouldn't paper a room at all, but would paint it.

"You *must* paper it," said the gentleman, rather warmly.

"You must paper it," said Thomas Gradgrind, "whether you like it or not. Don't tell *us* you wouldn't paper it. What do you mean, boy?"

"I'll explain to you, then, " said the gentleman, after another and a dismal pause, "why you wouldn't paper a room with representations of horses. Do you ever see horses walking up and down the sides of rooms in reality — in fact? Do you?"

"Yes, Sir!" from one half. "No, Sir!" from the other.

"Of course, No," said the gentleman, with an indignant look at the wrong half. "Why, then, you are not to see anywhere, what you don't see in fact; you are not to have anywhere, what you don't have in fact."

(BOOK I, CHAP. 2)

This kind of wild, Alice-in-Wonderland quality pervades life in Coketown, and the confusion of real horses and pictures of horses is symptomatic of the linguistic dislocations to which Coketowners are subjected. They live in a world where the landscape of actuality is constantly remade by verbal bulldozing. People are told what the words they use *really* mean, and the basic relationships between verbal symbols and reality are confused or blatantly ignored. Coketown becomes a kind of circus of linguistic wonders where irresponsible verbal juggling and acrobatics continually cheapen the value of language.

The arbitrary authoritarianism of Mr. Gradgrind's rebuke to the boy who would paint rather than paper his room recalls Alice's disorienting encounters with Humpty Dumpty, who says, "When *I* use a word . . . it means just what I choose it to mean — neither more nor less." It is, he says, a matter of "which is to be master — that's all." And in Coketown, words are not allowed to get away with a thing. A horse is to be known only in the most dismally factual way: "Quadruped. Graminivorous. Forty teeth, namely twenty-four grinders, four eyeteeth, and twelve incisive. Sheds coat in the spring; in marshy countries, sheds hoofs, too. Hoofs hard, but requiring to be shod with iron. Age known by marks in mouth" (book 1, chap. 2). With Humpty-Dumpty-like logic, Mr. Gradgrind tells Sissy Jupe that "Sissy is not a name. . . . Don't call yourself Sissy. Call yourself Cecilia" (book 1, chap. 2). Similarly, the school inspector tells the "little pitchers" at Gradgrind's school that "What is called Taste, is only another name for Fact" (book 1, chap. 2). Bounderby engages in the same kind of verbal highhandedness in talking to Stephen Blackpool: "Ah! *I* know what you said; more than that, I know what you mean, you see. Not always the same thing, by the Lord Harry! Quite different things" (book 2, chap. 5). In Coketown words, as well as people, are bullied.

Hard Times is also full of verbal fantasizing that distorts and disregards the normal relationship of words to the things they stand for. Mr. Bounderby's reaction to the robbery of his bank is characteristic. Although he lost only one hundred and fifty pounds, "what might have been" is his only concern: "It might have been twenty thousand pound," he says, or it might have been "twice twenty. There's no knowing what it would have been, or wouldn't have been, as it was, but for the fellows' being disturbed" (book 2, chap. 8). Bounderby prefers to believe — and have everyone else believe — that the reality was calamitous. A more elaborate confusion of words and reality is the game Bounderby plays with his past. His whole identity turns out to be a verbal fraud. "I passed the day in a ditch, and the night in a pigsty," he tells Mrs. Gradgrind. "That's the way I spent my tenth birthday. Not that a ditch was new to me, for I was born in a ditch." He assures the "stunned" Mrs. Gradgrind that he "was so ragged and dirty, that you wouldn't have touched me with a pair of tongs." The villain he has invented to support this role is a grandmother: "the wickedest and the worst old woman that ever lived. If I got a little pair of shoes by any chance, she would take 'em off and sell 'em for drink. Why, I have known that grandmother of mine lie in her bed and drink her four-teen glasses of liquor before breakfast!" (book 1, chap. 4). Actually these colorful deprivations bear no resemblance to the prosaic reality of his humble but wholesome village childhood.

Mrs. Sparsit, Bounderby's housekeeper, plays similar games. Her one claim to distinction is, in fact, a purely verbal one: her husband was a "Powler." With this magic word she defines her world and tries to impress all comers: she even tries by force of it to rise above circumstance. And like Bounderby's, Mrs. Sparsit's identity is based upon a verbal fraud perpetrated largely by her employer with her tacit approval and occasional assistance. Bounderby, Dickens observes, has "brightened Mrs. Sparsit's juvenile career with every possible advantage, and showered waggon-loads of early roses all over that lady's path" (book 1, chap. 7).

> "Why, what do *you* know about tumblers? [asks Bounderby.] At the time when, to have been a tumbler in the mud of

the streets, would have been a godsend to me, a prize in the lottery to me, you were at the Italian Opera. You were coming out of the Italian Opera, ma'am, in white satin and jewels, a blaze of splendour, when I hadn't a penny to buy a link to light you."

"I certainly, Sir," returned Mrs. Sparsit, with a dignity serenely mournful, "was familiar with the Italian Opera at a very early age."

_ "But you must confess that you were born in the lap of luxury, yourself. Come, ma'am, you know you were born in the lap of luxury."

"I do not, Sir," returned Mrs. Sparsit with a shake of her head, "deny it."

"And you were in crack society. Devilish high society," he said, warming his legs.

"It is true, Sir," returned Mrs. Sparsit, with an affectation of humility the very opposite of his, and therefore in no danger of jostling it.

"You were in the tiptop fashion, and all the rest of it," said Mr. Bounderby.

"Yes, Sir," returned Mrs. Sparsit, with a kind of social widowhood upon her. "It is unquestionably true."

(BOOK I, CHAP. 7)

The verbal irresponsibility of games like these which Mr. Bounderby and Mrs. Sparsit play does not matter a great deal, for others are not seriously affected. More disturbing are the activities of another fictionalizer, Harthouse's brother, the M. P. He exercises his talents in the House of Commons, where his

happy turn of humour . . . had told immensely . . . on the occasion of his entertaining it with his (and the Board of Directors') view of a railway accident, in which the most careful officers ever known, employed by the most liberal managers ever heard of, assisted by the finest mechanical contrivances ever devised, the whole in action on the best line ever constructed, had killed five people and wounded thirty-two, by a casualty without which the excellence of the whole system would have been positively incomplete. Among the slain was a cow, and among the scattered articles unowned, a

> widow's cap. And the honourable member had so tickled the
> House (which has a delicate sense of humour) by putting the
> cap on the cow, that it became impatient of any serious
> reference to the Coroner's Inquest, and brought the railway
> off with Cheers and Laughter.
>
> (BOOK 2, CHAP. 2)

This charming levity masks human tragedy, callous feeling, and social irresponsibility.

When Bounderby's workers rather than his childhood are the subject of his verbal fantasies, the game becomes still more dangerous. For in the case of Stephen Blackpool, Bounderby acts, with disastrous consequences, upon a false and purely verbal reality that he helps to create and perpetuate. The prevailing fictions shared by the mill owners dismiss the hands as a "bad lot" — never thankful, always restless, never knowing what they want. They live upon the best: buying fresh butter, insisting upon Mocha coffee, and rejecting all but prime parts of meat. Yet the hands are "eternally dissatisfied and unmanageable" (book 1, chap. 5), and Bounderby is convinced that they all want to "be set up in a coach and six, and to be fed on turtle soup and venison, with a gold spoon" (book 1, chap. 11). Moreover, he views mill work as "the pleasantest . . . lightest . . . best-paid work there is," and insists it could not be improved "unless we laid down Turkey carpets on the floors" (book 2, chap. 2). "Show me a dissatisfied Hand," says Bounderby, "and I'll show you a man that's fit for anything bad, I don't care what it is" (book 2, chap. 8). Against this deadly linguistic con game, Stephen has no chance.

The catastrophes of the novel are generated not only by this kind of verbal self-deception but by other kinds of verbal irresponsibility as well. It is, for example, the verbal chicanery of Slackbridge, the union organizer, that helps turn the mill hands against Stephen Blackpool. Slackbridge's florid rhetoric also creates a fantasy world, one of "downtrodden operatives" who are slaves of "an iron-handed and a grinding despotism" (book 2, chap. 4). Instead of rich food from a gold spoon and a coach and six, Slackbridge pictures his "prostrate friends" as living "with the galling yoke of tyrants on your necks and the iron foot of despotism treading down your fallen forms into the dust of the earth, upon which right glad would your oppressors be to see you creeping on your bellies all the days of your lives, like the serpent in the garden." Instead of fresh butter, Mocha coffee, and prime cuts of meat, Slackbridge sees "hard but honest beds . . . made in toil, and . . . scanty but in-dependent pots . . . boiled in hardship" (book 3, chap. 4). Slackbridge's rhetoric is as dishonest as Bounderby's fictions, and his language is no more trustworthy. Bounderby turns Stephen into a "man that's fit for anything bad." Slackbridge makes him a "viper" and a "dastard craven."

A more subtle form of dishonesty is found in the language of James Harthouse, the political dilettante. His cynicism, like Slackbridge's rhetoric or Bounderby's fantasies, undermines honest communication. To Bounderby the mill hands are a "bad lot"; to Slackbridge they are "prostrate sons of labor." To the bored and uncommitted Harthouse, they are "members of the fluffy classes," a condescendingly comic term that degrades beneath a mask of cleverness. The glib Harthouse as-sumes a calculated candidness that is quite disarming. He "goes in" for Gradgrind's opinions "because I have no choice of opinions, and may as well back them as anything else." "I have not so much as the slightest predilection left," he tells Louisa. "I assure you I attach not the least im-portance to any opinions . . . any set of ideas will do just as much good as any other set, and just as much harm as any other set." It is an attrac-tively insidious stance. As Dickens observes, "This vicious assumption of honesty in dishonesty—a vice so dangerous, so deadly, and so common" (book 2, chap. 2) holds an almost irresistable charm for Louisa.

Mr. Gradgrind with his statistical blue books perpetuates still another kind of verbal distortion. His linguistic failing is abstraction—the use of language that is so divorced from particulars that it reports no more honestly than Bounderby's fantasies. In Mr. Gradgrind's study, Dickens says, "the most complicated social questions were cast up, got into exact totals, and finally settled—if those concerned could only have been brought to know it." Like an astronomer arranging "the starry universe solely by pen, ink, and paper," Mr. Gradgrind "had no need to cast an eye upon the teeming myriads of human beings around him, but could settle all their destinies on a slate, and wipe out all their tears with one dirty little bit of sponge" (book 1, chap. 15). When she visits Stephen's lodgings, Louisa finally begins to sense the basic dishonesty of her father's bird's-eye view of humanity:

> For the first time in her life Louisa had come into one of the
> dwellings of the Coketown Hands; for the first time in her life
> she was face to face with anything like individuality in connex-
> ion with them. She knew of their existence by hundreds

and by thousands. She knew what results in work a given number of them would produce in a given space of time. She knew them in crowds passing to and from their nests, like ants or beetles. But she knew from her reading infinitely more of the ways of toiling insects than of these toiling men and women.

Something to be worked so much and paid so much, and there ended; something to be infallibly settled by laws of supply and demand; something that blundered against those laws, and floundered into difficulty; something that was a little pinched when wheat was dear, and over-ate itself when wheat was cheap; something that increased at such a rate of percentage, and yielded such another percentage of crime, and such another percentage of pauperism; something wholesale, of which vast fortunes were made; something that occasionally rose like a sea, and did some harm and waste (chiefly to itself), and fell again; this she knew the Coketown Hands to be. But, she had scarcely thought more of separating them into units, than of separating the sea itself into its component drops.

(BOOK 2, CHAP. 6)

In the absence of human contacts, people are reduced to abstractions and statistics. There can be no real understanding in such cases, and up goes one more barrier to communication.

Still another potentially dangerous linguistic practice presented in *Hard Times* is the attempt to control events by simple assertion. As a "lady" Mrs. Sparsit cannot allow herself the indignity of being an employee, and so she denies the fact and maintains her station by a bit of verbal legerdemain. When Bounderby, with his wedding approaching, suggests that she remove to the bank on the same "terms" of employment, Mrs. Sparsit interrupts: "I beg your pardon, Sir. You were so good as to promise that you would always substitute the phrase, annual compliment" (book 1, chap. 16). As an avid word magician himself, Mr. Bounderby complies. Similarly, though Mrs. Sparsit pries relentlessly into the affairs of young Tom Gradgrind, she keeps herself honest with more verbal sleight-of-hand: "No, Bitzer," she says to her informer, "say an individual, and I will hear you; say Mr. Thomas, and you must excuse me" (book 2, chap. 1). Such strategies are almost a way of life for Mrs. Sparsit, but she is not the sole practitioner of word magic. Mrs.

Gradgrind, having caught her children "wondering," blames Tom for leading Louisa astray. Louisa denies Tom's participation only to be stopped by her mother: "Louisa, don't tell me, in my state of health; for unless you had been encouraged, it is morally and physically impossible that you could have done it" (book 1, chap. 8). Even "the eminently practical" Mr. Gradgrind, in an effort to assure the invincibility of his system of childrearing, resorts to this device. Having discovered the mathematical Thomas and the metallurgical Louisa peeping under the circus tent, he is distressed that children raised with such "mathematical exactness" and so "replete with facts" could even momentarily fall from a state of statistical grace. When Louisa explains her action by saying she is tired — "I don't know of what — of everything, I think" — Mr. Gradgrind replies, "Say not another word. . . . You are childish, I will hear no more" (book 1, chap. 3).

It is through the gradual accumulation of such linguistic behavior that Dickens reveals Coketown to be a place of verbal surrealism. There language has become so unreliable that it finally is an impediment to understanding and a means of victimizing people. Stephen Blackpool begins to understand this in the course of his second interview with Bounderby:

> Look how you considers of us, and writes of us, and talks of us, and goes up wi' yor deputations to Secretaries 'o State 'bout us, and how yo are awlus right, and how we are awlus wrong, and never had'n no reason in us sin ever we were born. Look how this ha' growen an' growen, Sir, bigger an' bigger, broader an' broader, harder an' harder, fro year to year, fro generation unto generation. Who can look on 't, Sir, and fairly tell a man 'tis not a muddle?
>
> (BOOK 2, CHAP. 5)

Rachael, too, is confounded by her inability to understand and by her misgivings about the reliability not only of people's actions but of their words as well. In her distress and despair and echoing Louisa's own sense of the gap between herself and the operators, she says to Louisa:

> O young lady, young lady . . . I hope you may be [sorry], but I don't know! I can't say what you may ha' done! The like of you don't know us, don't care for us, don't belong to us. I am not sure why you may ha' come that night. I can't tell but what you may ha' come wi' some aim of your own, not mindin

to what trouble you brought such as the poor lad. I said then,
Bless you for coming; and I said it of my heart, you seemed to
take so pitifully to him; but I don't know now, I don't know!

(BOOK 3, CHAP. 4)

Stephen and Rachael, as two of its most likely victims, have a
stronger sense of the linguistic dislocation of their world and of its consequences than their betters do. At the end of his life, Stephen, a primary
victim, sees with perfect clarity the two main sources of breakdown in
his affairs:

> If aw th' things that tooches us, my dear, was not so muddled,
> I should'n ha' had'n need to coom heer. If we was not in a
> muddle among ourseln, I should'n ha' been, by my own
> fellow weavers and workin' brothers, so mistook. If Mr.
> Bounderby had ever know'd me right — if he'd ever know'd me
> a aw — he would'n ha' took'n offence wi' me. He would'n ha'
> suspect'n me.

(BOOK 3, CHAP. 6)

Stephen's case is a significant index of the centrality of communication
as an issue in the book. Much of his story deals with the breakdown of
communication and its consequences. And the undeserved decline in his
fortunes is marked by the change that occurs from the beginning of his
first interview with Bounderby to the end of his last — at which point the
breakdown in communication is complete. When Stephen first presents
himself, Bounderby, quite truthfully if a little unfairly, remarks to him,
"we have never had any difficulty with you, and you have never been
one of the unreasonable ones" (book 1, chap. 11). But at the end of the
second interview, Bounderby characterizes the essentially unchanged
Stephen as "a waspish, raspish, ill-conditioned chap" and "one of those
chaps who have always got a grievance" (book 2, chap. 5).

But the consequences of lack of understanding and failures in communication are not confined to victimized operatives. They pervade the
action of the book. Some are trivial; others, very serious. Some are comic; others, pathetic. Purely comic are the minor misfortunes that
envelop Mrs. Sparsit and finally condemn her to the purgatory of life as
the companion of the obese and peevish Lady Scadgers. It is through a
kind of failure in communication that Mrs. Sparsit brings her world
down about her ears. She is caught by a downpour in the act of eaves-
dropping on Louisa and Harthouse, and the upshot of their hurried

meeting is lost to her in "an unavoidable halo of confusion and indistinctness" (book 2, chap. 11). Mistakenly believing herself the bearer of scandalous and sensational tidings, she hurries off to confusion and disgrace with what Bounderby characterizes as "a Cock-and-a-Bull" (book 3, chap. 3). But Mrs. Sparsit does not learn and compounds her humiliation by producing Mrs. Pegler, Bounderby's mother. Once again, she is the victim of failure in communication, as Mrs. Pegler reminds her: "I told this lady over and over again," she says to her son, "that I knew she was doing what would not be agreeable to you, but she would do it" (book 3, chap. 5).

The plight of Mrs. Gradgrind is both comic and pathetic. Hers is an existence of completely collapsed communication. Her life is of little consequence to anyone, and she has lived for years without even attempting to communicate, a victim finally of verbal bullying. "You must remember, my dear," she says on her deathbed to Louisa, "that whenever I have said anything, on any subject, I have never heard the last of it: and consequently, that I have long left off saying anything." The seriocomic irony of her final act underscores the importance of human communication as a theme in the book. She dies making a fancied but futile effort to communicate one final time with her husband, passing to the next world tracing what Dickens calls "figures of wonderful no-meaning" (book 2, chap. 9). The phrase perfectly describes the linguistic abuses that characterize the world of Coketown.

Comedy also relieves the seriousness of the theme as it is worked out in Bounderby. He is not to be faulted merely for falsifying language. His whole being, in fact, is an impenetrable obstacle to communication. He refuses to believe Rachael's account of Louisa's visit to Stephen Blackpool, and when it is corroborated, he only grudgingly hears it (book 3, chap. 4). When Louisa has returned to her father's house, Gradgrind says to her husband, "Bounderby, I see reason to doubt whether we have ever quite understood Louisa." "Who do you mean by We?" blusters Bounderby (book 3, chap. 3). With a closed mind he continues:

> "I know the Hands of this town. I know 'em all pretty well. They're real. When a man tells me anything about imaginative qualities, I always tell that man, whoever he is, that I know what he means. He means turtle soup and venison, with a gold spoon, and that he wants to be set up with a coach and six. That's what your daughter wants."
>
> (BOOK 3, CHAP. 3)

And when Gradgrind protests that he is being "unreasonable," Bounder-by replies with obstinate illogicality: "I am glad to hear you say so. Because when Tom Gradgrind, with his new lights, tells me that what I say is unreasonable, I am convinced at once it must be devilish sensible" (book 3, chap. 3). But the comic absurdity of such a "self-made Hum-bug" (book 3, chap. 5) only thinly disguises the dangerousness of his bull-headed refusal to hear what others are saying.

Pointing to one of the most important thematic relationships in the novel, Dickens asks, "Is it possible, I wonder, that there was any analogy between the case of the Coketown population and the case of the little Gradgrinds?" (book 1, chap. 5). There is, of course, an important parallel, and in many ways the most affecting of the consequences of verbal breakdown are those which afflict the Gradgrind household, where relationships between parents and children deteriorate. We have already referred to Mrs. Gradgrind's verbal alienation from her family. Little is said of the origins of young Tom's problems, though Dickens makes it clear that he is a victim both of his upbringing and of innate weakness of character. However, in questioning Louisa about Tom, Harthouse perceptively points to part of Tom's trouble — what Hart-house refers to as Tom's lack of "advantages":

> "Whether — forgive my plainness — whether any great amount of confidence is likely to have been established be-tween himself and his most worthy father."
>
> "I do not," said Louisa, flushing with her own great remembrance in that wise, "think it likely."
>
> "Or, between himself, and — I may trust to your perfect understanding of my meaning, I am sure — and his highly esteemed brother-in-law."
>
> She flushed deeper and deeper, and was burning red when she replied in a fainter voice, "I do not think that likely, either."
>
> (BOOK 2, CHAP. 7)

Harthouse is quite right in suggesting that the failure of Gradgrind's system of child-rearing turns, in part, upon failures to establish lines of communication and that this is part of young Tom's problems.

But it is in terms of Louisa and her father that the flawed relation-ships between parent and child and the failures they produce are most fully and graphically developed. Though not all of the misfortunes which beset the unhappy Gradgrind family stem from this source, it is an important contributing factor. That it is centrally important in the story of the Gradgrinds is stressed by the parallel Dickens establishes between Stephen Blackpool and Mr. Gradgrind. Louisa's return to her father's house collapses his world and plunges him figuratively into a pit. Indeed, he talks of his sense of the ground giving way under him. The crisis also forces him to an agonizing reappraisal and — like Stephen — to the conclusion that a failure in understanding is at the root of his trouble: "I appear to myself to have become better informed as to Louisa's character, than in previous years. The enlightenment has been painfully forced upon me, and the discovery is not mine" (book 3, chap. 3). Like Stephen, he is, through his misfortunes, forced to an awareness of the problems and an understanding of the barriers to communication that have entrapped him.

The most dramatic depiction of the Gradgrinds' inability to communicate is the scene in which Louisa's father proposes that she marry Bounderby. The tragedy of total misunderstanding between a father and his favorite child is heightened by the fact that they are repeatedly on the verge of a breakthrough. Mr. Gradgrind begins and then waits "as if he would have been glad that she said something" (book 1, chap. 15), but she says nothing. Later the right moment passes once again:

> From the beginning, she had sat looking at him fixedly. As he now leaned back in his chair, and bent his deep-set eyes upon her in his turn, perhaps he might have seen one wavering moment in her, when she was impelled to throw herself upon his breast, and give him the pent-up confidences of her heart. But, to see it, he must have overleaped at a bound the artificial barriers he had for many years been erecting, between himself and all those subtle essences of humanity which will elude the utmost cunning of algebra until the last trumpet ever to be sounded shall blow even algebra to wreck. The barriers were too many and too high for such a leap. With his unbending, utilitarian, matter-of-fact face, he hardened her again; and the moment shot away into the plumbless depths of the past, to mingle with all the lost opportunities that are drowned there.

Recalling this day after she has left her husband's house, Louisa senses not only these narrowly missed opportunities but their unhappy consequences as well. "What has risen to my lips now," she tells her heartsick father, "would have risen to my lips then, if you had given me a moment's help. I don't reproach you, father. What you have never nurtured in me, you have never nurtured in yourself; but O! if you had only done so, long ago, or if you had only neglected me, what a much better and much happier creature I should have been this day!" (book 2, chap. 12). It is the essence of Dickens's story, of course, that understanding should not come until it is too late.

The proposal scene stresses the importance of communication in another way, for, interestingly, the failures that occur are partly the result of verbal subtleties and are, therefore, linguistic in origin. For instance, when Louisa asks whether Mr. Bounderby expects her to love him, Gradgrind engages in an elaborate but evasive display of semantic acrobatics with the word "love" in which, finally, "fanciful," "fantastic," and "sentimental" all become synonyms. He concludes by observing that "the expression itself — I merely suggest to you, my dear — may be a little misplaced," and proceeds to consider the match as a matter of "tangible Fact." Subsequently, Louisa makes the mistake of speaking metaphorically to her matter-of-fact father in a speech that both comments on the life she had led and foreshadows the future action of the story. Staring out at the gloomy prospect of Coketown, she says: "There seems to be nothing there but languid and monotonous smoke. Yet when the night comes, Fire bursts out, father!" But with utilitarian obtuseness, Gradgrind merely replies: "Of course I know that Louisa. I do not see the application of the remark." Irony as well as metaphor proves a barrier to communication. The scene ends with Louisa ironically reminding her father about the unnaturalness of her childhood: "You have dealt so wisely with me, father, from my cradle to this hour, that I never had a child's belief or a child's fear." He completely mistakes the tone of her statement: "Mr. Gradgrind was quite moved by his success, and by this testimony to it. 'My dear Louisa,' said he, 'you abundantly repay my care. Kiss me, my dear girl.'"

Such recurring failures to communicate are underscored with an especially effective irony. Louisa makes a futile effort to express with complete honesty to her father — and through him to Mr. Bounderby — her attitude toward marriage.

> "Mr. Bounderby," she went on in a steady, straight way . . .
> "asks me to marry him. The question I have to ask myself is, shall I marry him? That is so, father, is it not? You have told me so, father. Have you not?"
> "Certainly, my dear."
> "Let it be so. Since Mr. Bounderby likes to take me thus, I am satisfied to accept his proposal. Tell him, father, as soon as

you please, that this was my answer. Repeat it, word for word,
if you can, because I should wish him to know what I said."

Despite her scrupulous care to be clear and exact — an effort for which her
father in fact commends her — Louisa's point is not, of course, really
understood. And so the episode ends in failure. The matters never really
communicated finally come clear only in the catastrophe that envelops
Louisa toward the end of the novel. When it is too late, Gradgrind says to
his daughter:

> "I will not say, Louisa, that if you had by any happy chance
> undeceived me some time ago, it would have been better for us
> both; better for your peace, and better for mine. For I am sensi-
> ble that it may not have been a part of my system to invite any
> confidence of that kind. I had proved my — my system to
> myself, and I have rigidly administered it; and I must bear the
> responsibility of its failures. I only entreat you to believe, my
> favourite child, that I have meant to do right."
>
> (BOOK 3, CHAP. I)

The poignancy of this admission is only intensified by the fact that Louisa
had tried, to no avail, to do just what he asks.

Louisa's relationship with her father is not the only one blighted by
lack of communication. Not surprisingly, her marital mismatch is a study
in noncommunication. Mrs. Sparsit's return to Bounderby's household
after the robbery at the bank creates one situation in which this problem is
thrown into dramatic relief. The matter of Mrs. Sparsit's resuming her
former duties at the teapot becomes, for example, the focal point of a painful scene in which the inability of husband and wife to speak honestly to
each other concludes with Louisa remarking to her husband: "'You are in-
comprehensible this morning. . . . Pray take no further trouble to explain
yourself. I am not curious to know your meaning. What does it matter?'"
(book 2, chap. 9). Much has been left unsaid in their exchange, and
frustration and unhappiness obviously lurk just below the surface and guilt
and bitterness only a little deeper.

Louisa not only cuts herself off from her father and her husband. She
suddenly brings to an end her initially promising relationship with Sissy
Jupe. Sensing Sissy's wonder, pity, sorrow, and doubt at the announcement of her impending marriage to Bounderby, Louisa "from that moment . . . was impassive, proud and cold — held Sissy at a distance
— [was] changed to her altogether." Ironically, Louisa is even unable to

communicate with her brother, the one person she really cares about. Sensing that Tom may be involved at the affair at the bank — or at least that he knows more about it than he is saying — Louisa determines to approach him and goes to his room, where she finds him feigning sleep. At last he pretends to awaken and asks what is the matter:

> "Tom, have you anything to tell me? If ever you loved me in your life, and have anything concealed from every one besides, tell it to me."
>
> "I don't know what you mean, Loo. You have been dreaming."
>
> "My dear brother. . . . Is there nothing you can tell me if you will? You can tell me nothing that will change me. O Tom, tell me the truth!"
>
> "I don't know what you mean, Loo!"
>
> (BOOK 2, CHAP. 8)

And though she persists, there is nothing. Finally, like Stephen Blackpool and like her father, Louisa is a victim of breakdowns in communication.

In important ways, then, *Hard Times* is about failure in communication. It dramatizes a concern Dickens expressed in a speech in Birmingham in 1853. Speaking of education for working men, he observed that "in this world a great deal of the bitterness among us arises from an imperfect understanding of one another." He urged "the bringing together of employers and employed" and the creation "of a better common understanding among those whose interests are identical." In *Hard Times,* as in this speech, Dickens is concerned with the link between communication and community. Communication is essential to the development of relationships between individuals. Its absense is a chief source of flaws and failures in these relationships. The book's implications, of course, go beyond the personal level, for the verbal muddle at the heart of *Hard Times* ultimately helps undermine social relationships and responsibilities. Manipulation and distortion of language destroy people collectively as well as individually, and so the verbal barriers that keep individuals at odds also breed social disorder.

To read *Hard Times* from this point of view is not, of course, to perceive the only insight into social issues that Dickens offers in the book. His keen sense of the ills that afflict society is articulated in more than one way. But to approach the book as one which deals importantly with problems of communication and understanding is to approach it in a way that is readily accessible to readers familiar with the excesses of modern advertising and propaganda, with Newspeak, and with credibility gaps. As a novel that depicts with force and clarity Dickens's perception of verbal muddle and irresponsibility and its personal and social consequences, *Hard Times* adds an important insight into what ails society to those embodied in the sequence of social novels that begins with *Bleak House*.

Polyphony and Problematic in *Hard Times*

Roger Fowler

The polarization of critical response to *Hard Times* is familiar enough to make detailed reporting unnecessary, but since this polarization is a fact relevant to my argument, I will recapitulate it briefly.

Popular reception of the novel has been largely antagonistic or uninterested. The character of the earlier novels has led to the formation of a cheerful and sentimental "Dickensian" response which finds *Hard Times,* like the other later novels, cold and uncomfortable, lacking in the innocent jollity, sentimentality and grotesquery of the earlier writings. When Dickens's anniversary was mentioned in a T.V. spot on February 7, 1983, the novelist was identified through a list of his works which totally excluded the later "social" novels.

In other circles, there has been a keenly appreciative response to *Hard Times:* in some quarters more academic, and in some quarters more socialist. Committedly positive evaluation is found as early as 1860 in Ruskin and then in this century in Shaw, whose appreciation of the book as "serious social history" initiated a line of evaluation more recently reflected in, for example, Raymond Williams and in David Craig. Then there is a famous and extravagant essay by Leavis:

> Of all Dickens's works it is the one that has all the strength of
> his genius, together with a strength no other of them can show
> —that of a completely serious work of art.

From *The Changing World of Charles Dickens,* edited by Robert Giddings. © 1983 by Vision Press Ltd. Vision Press and Barnes & Noble Books, 1983.

If Leavis was overenthusiastic, others, some such as John Holloway and David M. Hirsch provoked by Leavis's surplus of commen-
dation, have insisted on faults in the novel both as art and as social
history. Even that majority of modern academic critics who accept and
praise *Hard Times* concede some faults. Among the flaws cited by both
camps are the following. A failure of a documentary kind is the presentation of the demagogue Slackbridge — "a mere figment of the middle-
class imagination. No such man would be listened to by a meeting of
English factory hands" (Shaw). Similarly, the use of a professional circus
to represent Fancy as opposed to Fact has been faulted on the grounds
that Dickens might have found Fancy in the native recreations of working people (Craig). A more "ideological" criticism would allege that
Dickens's *concept* of Fancy was, judging from the symbols by which he
represented it, too trivial to weigh effectively against the Fact of
Utilitarian economic theory and philosophy of education (Holloway,
Lodge). Other critics have admitted faults of characterization — the girl
Sissy is sentimentally presented and emerges as inadequate: her childhood attributes do not ground her later strength on Louisa's behalf.
Again, Stephen and Rachael are said to be too good to be true; Stephen's
martyrdom to a drunken wife is a cliché; his refusal to join the union is
not motivated and therefore puts him into a weak, contradictory position in relation to his fellow-workers. Now these allegations of faults of
construction are not naive "Dickensian" complaints. There is real
evidence that many things are not quite right with the book, for
whatever reason: because of the unfamiliar constraints of small-scale
writing for weekly parts, because of the secondhand nature of Dickens's
experience?

Since *Hard Times* has gained a very positive reputation in this century, we should beware of condemning it by totting up "faults." Perhaps
the yardstick which we unconsciously apply, the tradition of the
humanistic novel already well established by 1850, is not entirely relevant. It might be preferable to revise our conception of what type of
novel this is, or at least to suspend preconception. *Hard Times* is problematic for the critics, and that response itself is perhaps evidence of
peculiarities of form. And what we know about the genesis of the novel
suggests that it was problematic for Dickens too, involving him in compositional innovations. By this I do not refer merely to the structural
consequences of weekly serialization (a discipline he had experienced
only once before, in writing *Barnaby Rudge* [1841]), though this mode undoubtedly imposed constraints on episodic and thematic structure, and

demanded compression. I mean by "compositional innovations" new and defamiliarizing dispositions of language in response to new themes and unprecedented *and unresolved* ideological complexity.

A possible model for the structure of *Hard Times* is provided by Mikhail Bakhtin's theory of the "polyphonic" novel [in *Problems of Dostoyevsky's Poetics*]; a theory which has the great benefit, for my purpose, of being interpretable in linguistic terms. In a complex argument, partly theoretical and partly historical, Bakhtin proposes that there have existed two modes of representational fiction: monologic on the one hand and polyphonic or dialogic on the other. The monologic novel, which he claims has been the dominant traditional form, is authoritarian in essence: the author insists on the particular ideology which he voices, and the characters are "objectified," dependent on the authorial position, and evaluated from the point of view of that position. In the polyphonic novel, on the other hand, the characters (or the "hero," according to Bakhtin) are more liberated: they achieve voices, and points of view, which challenge the validity of the authorial position. The musical metaphor of polyphony refers to the copresence of independent but interconnected voices. "Dialogue" means implicit dialogue, not turn-by-turn speeches: it refers to the fact that one person's speech-forms reflect consciousness of the actual or potential response of an interlocutor, orientation towards a second act of speech. But there is a stronger meaning which Bakhtin seems to have in mind for "dialogic," and that is "dialectical." The dialogic relationship confronts unresolved contrary ideologies, opposing voices in which conflicting worldviews resist submersion or cancellation. The dialectical nature of Bakhtin's aesthetic can best be seen in his discussion of *carnival* [in *Rabelais and His World*], which was in his view the medieval forerunner of the polyphonic novel. Carnival, with its boy kings and other multifarious travesties, mediates opposites, associates them while preserving their autonomous identities. It rejoices in extremes, negation, inversion, subversion, antithesis. The rhetorical figures generated by the logic of carnival are clear: they include prominently hyperbole, litotes, negation, syntactic inversions, paradox, contradiction. In social terms, the carnivalistic dialectic is the tension between mutually supportive but antithetical partners such as ruler and subject, employer and worker, teacher and pupil, husband and wife. And we would expect these differences of role, and antagonisms, to be articulated in the language of carnivalistic structures.

At a superficial level, the application of these ideas to *Hard Times* seems well justified. Three of the role-clashes just mentioned (employer/

worker, teacher / pupil, husband / wife) figure directly and importantly in the plot. Then the novel contains a large number of diverse characters and groups of characters of very different social origins and affiliations, putting forward many and clashing points of view. The circus performers are an almost literal case of carnival: their diversity and deviance are strongly emphasized as is their challenge to the authority of Gradgrind and Bounderby (book 1, chap. 6). But polyphonic or dialogic structure is by no means limited to these circus artistes, but exists in the ensemble of numerous voices of opinion and conflict: Slackbridge, Bounderby, Stephen Blackpool, Harthouse, Louisa, Sissy, etc. The task for the analyst who wishes to make sense of this medley of voices is twofold. First, it is necessary to show in detail the linguistic and semiotic characteristics of the various voices (including the narrating voice) which participate in the dialogic structure. Second, the polyphonic structure, the multiplicity of voices, needs to be interpreted in terms of the author's ideology. A plurality of voices does not in itself mean a nonauthoritarian narrative stance.

Turning to language itself, Bakhtin does not give a very clear guide as to how the structure of language contributes to the dialogic aesthetic. In fact, he appears to be quite negative on the dialogic value of stylistic variety. But this caution is strategic. He has to concede that Dostoyevsky, his main subject, is stylistically flat, but he must claim, of course, that his thesis works even in this linguistically undifferentiated case. He observes that marked linguistic individuation of fictional characters may lead to an impression of closure, a feeling that the author has definitively analysed a character and placed a boundary around its imaginative or moral potential: "characters' linguistic differentiation and clear-cut 'characteristics of speech' have the greatest significance precisely for the creation of objectivized, finalized images of people." This seems to me not so much a limitation as an illumination, specifically an insight into our response to Dickens's grotesques: Peggotty, Micawber, Mrs. Gamp, and here, Slackbridge. All such characters seem to be clearly delineated, completely known, striking but uncomplicated. But we also need Bakhtin's more positive concession concerning the dialogic potential of speech styles; this potential is effective under certain conditions:

> the point is not the mere presence of specific styles, social dialects, etc., . . . the point is the dialogical *angle* at which they . . . are juxtaposed or counterposed in the work.

and

dialogical relationships are possible among linguistic styles, social dialects, etc., if those phenomena are perceived as semantic positions, as a sort of linguistic *Weltanschauung*.

That is to say, speech styles need not be just caricaturing oddities, but to transcend caricature they must encode characters' worldviews as dialectical alternatives to the worldview of the author and/or, I would suggest, other characters. Thus we might investigate whether, say, Stephen Blackpool's speech, or Bounderby's, encodes in its specific linguistic form a worldview, a set of attitudes; and how the two attitudes relate — in this case, antithetically. Similarly, and perhaps easier to demonstrate, we can look at the dialogic relationships between Gradgrind and Sleary on the one hand, and Gradgrind and the author on the other.

How to proceed in this project? The examples just mentioned are merely striking instances of many, perhaps dozens of semiotically significant stylistic oppositions which permeate *Hard Times*. To provide a full account would require a book, not a chapter. As essential as space, however, is analytic methodology. Bakhtin provides no tools for analysing linguistic structure, but there is one linguistic theory which explicitly covers Bakhtin's condition that speech styles should be treated as embodying worldviews: M. A. K. Halliday's "functional" theory of language. I must send my readers elsewhere for details [to *Halliday: System and Function in Language* and *Language as Social Semiotic*], but Halliday's main premise is that linguistic varieties within a community, or "registers," encode different kinds of meaning, different orientations on experience. Halliday offers a number of analytic systems such as "transitivity," "mood," "cohesion," "information structure" which I and others have found very valuable in analysing texts for the worldviews which they embody. I will use some of these categories below, but my analysis is constrained by space to be largely untechnical.

A list of distinct speech styles in the novel would show that there is an exceptional range of clearly differentiated voices: Sissy, Sleary, Slackbridge, Harthouse, Childers, Bounderby, Stephen, Gradgrind, etc. The length and diversity of the list are of less importance than the specific meanings of the voices and of their structural relationships, but sheer diversity is of some significance for the notion of polyphony. It could be argued merely on the basis of this multiplicity and variousness of voices and people that *Hard Times* makes a *prima facie* claim to be a polyphonic novel. The case would be putative as a global observation, more concrete and demonstrable in relation to specific sections which are explicitly carnivalistic in conduct. The best instance of the latter is the scene at the Pegasus's Arms in book 1, chapter 6, when Gradgrind and Bounderby, in search of Sissy's father, are confronted by the members of the circus troupe, who speak "in a variety of voices" and who are combative and subversive in their address to these gentlemen. This scene, which is both challenging and farcical, threatens an anarchic overriding of utility and authority, and touches on antitheses which are more thoroughly debated elsewhere in the book.

I shall now look more closely at how the multiple languages of *Hard Times* signify and intersect by examining samples under three headings: *idiolect, sociolect,* and *dialogue.*

An idiolect is the characteristic speech style of an individual. Like dialect, it is a set of background features of language, supposedly constant and permanent characteristics which distinguish a person linguistically. In its most sophisticated realization it is the complex of features, mostly phonetic, by which we recognize our acquaintances' voices on the telephone. Now idiolects apply to literature in two ways. First, the elusive "style of an author" might be thought of as an idiolect. I mention this only to observe that *Hard Times* had no consistent authorial idiolect (unlike, to cite a comparable example, Mrs. Gaskell's *North and South*). Second, in fiction foregrounding of idiolect produces caricature; and although caricature is a fixing, objectifying process as Bakhtin has indicated, it is a device for making statements, and that is something we are looking for in *Hard Times*. The two sharp instances in this novel are the union demagogue Slackbridge and the circus-master Sleary. Each has a mode of speech which is quite idiosyncratic (with a qualification in the case of Sleary, below) and absolutely self-consistent.

Slackbridge conducts himself with a violent, biblical rhetoric:

> Oh my friends, the down-trodden operatives of Coketown! Oh my friends and fellow countrymen, the slave of an ironhanded and a grinding despotism! Oh my friends and fellow-sufferers, and fellow-workmen, and fellow-men! I tell you that the hour is come, when we must rally round one another as One united power, and crumble into dust the oppressors that too long have battened upon the plunder of our families, upon the sweat of our brows, upon the labour of our hands, upon the strength of our sinews, upon the God-created glorious rights of Humanity, and upon the holy and eternal privileges of Brotherhood!

It has been objected that no trades unionist of the time would have spoken like that (although apparently, this is not beyond question). But fidelity to the language of the delegates' platform is only part of the issue.

The point is that Dickens does not represent *any* social role in a focused way. He has created a symbolic language for his conception of "Slack-bridges," but this language signifies nothing precise: it is a generalized bombast which might inhabit the pulpit, the House of Lords, or any kind of political or public meeting. Conventionally, of course, this sort of language connotes vacuousness and insincerity, and presumably it does so here; but Slackbridge's appearance is an intervention in a complex moral dilemma (Stephen's refusal to "combine," and his subsequent ostracism by the workmates who know and respect him) and the signification of his speech style is inadequate to the situation. So Dickens is forced to comment directly on what Slackbridge represents:

> He was not so honest [as the assembled workmen], he was not so manly, he was not so good-humoured; he substituted cunning for their simplicity, and passion for their safe solid sense.

These judgements cannot be read off from the language in which Slackbridge is presented. His role remains puzzling, and since he is dramatically foregrounded as the main speaker against Stephen in this scene, the troubling nature of the scene (stemming largely from the unclarity of Stephen's motives and therefore of his relations with others at the meeting) remains provocatively unresolved.

Sleary is the second linguistic grotesque in the novel. Whereas Slackbridge's language is dominated by a bombastic rhetoric, Sleary's speech is submerged under brandy-and-water. Sibilants are drowned: [s, z, tʃ, ʃ, dʒ, ts] all reduce to a sound spelled *th*:

> Tho be it, my dear. (You thee how it ith, Thquire!) Farewell, Thethilia! My latht wordth to you ith thith, Thtick to the termth of your engagement, be obedient to the Thquire, and forget uth. But if, when you're grown up and married and well off, you come upon any horthe-riding ever, don't be hard upon it, don't be croth with it, give it a Bethspeak if you can, and think you might do wurth. People mutht be amuthed, Thquire, thomehow, . . . they can't be alwayth a working, nor yet they can't be alwayth a learning. Make the betht of uth; not the wortht.

But Sleary's function in the plot and in the thematic structure of the novel make him more than a comic drunk. In his first appearance (book 1, chap. 6), he is a firm leader of the circus-people in their challenge to the bullying of Gradgrind and Bounderby, and effectively presides over the passage of Sissy into the care of Gradgrind. At the end of the novel, he has been harbouring Gradgrind's criminal son Tom, and (carnivalistically, through the good offices of a dancing horse) manages Tom's flight from apprehension. He is then given virtually the last word, an almost verbatim repetition of the sentiment just quoted. His interventions in the story are directly implicated in Gradgrind's fortunes, and he is the philosophical antithesis to Gradgrind's utilitarian educational thesis: Sleary's Horse-Riding stands for Fancy. This notion of Fancy may well be too trivial for Dickens's purpose, as has been conceded; but at least Sleary is so constituted as to demand attention. The idiolect is insistently defamiliarizing: it "make[s] forms difficult . . . increase[s] the difficulty and length of perception" as Shklovsky puts it [in *Russian Formalist Criticism,* edited by Lee T. Lemon and Marion J. Reis]. It takes effort to determine what Sleary is saying because of the completeness and the whimsicality of the phonological transformation which has been applied to his speech. The reader is compelled to decipher a radical, and not entirely consistent, code which deforms everyday English words into momentarily unrecognizable spellings: *bitterth, prentitht.* These difficulties do not guarantee that what Sleary says is of any great interest; but the fact that Dickens has placed these difficulties in our way indicates that Sleary is *meant* to be listened to, that he is designed as a significant voice against Gradgrindism in the polyphonic structure of the book.

There is another interesting aspect of Sleary's speech, and one which further distinguishes his discourse from that of Slackbridge. Beneath the idiolect, there are markers which suggest a social dialect or sociolect. Dickens builds into Sleary's speech hints of working-class morphology and lexis: eathy (easily), ath (who), wouldn't . . . no more, took (taken), plain (plainly), winder, lyin', etc. (plus some odd spellings which suggest deviance from the middle-class code, but obscurely: natur, fortun, wurthst, conwenienth); and slang and oaths: morrithed (morrissed, "fled"), cut it short, damned, mith'd your tip (missed your tip, "jumped short"), cackler, pound ("wager"), etc. These characteristics link Sleary with the working class — in this novel, the interests of the "hands" — and with the circus fraternity — the spokespeople for Fancy. These links not only "naturalize" Sleary by providing him with social affiliations, but also broaden the basis of opposition to the Utilitarian philosophies embodied in Gradgrind (whom Sleary first meets in a confrontation).

The novel contains many other contrasts of speech style, and on the whole they can be explained sociolectally rather than idiolectally: Dickens seems to have accepted the principle that now provides the theoretical

basis for Hallidayan linguistics, namely that registers of language characterize social groups and encode their values. Consider, for example, the contrasting speech of Harthouse and of Stephen Blackpool. The former is first
introduced as an idle waster ("carelessly lounging") with a languid, verb-less,
fragmented speech (book 2, chap. 1). When he is established in Louisa's fa-
vours, however, this affectation is replaced by the syntax of "elaborated code":

> Mrs. Bounderby, though a graceless person, of the world
> worldly, I feel the utmost interest, I assure you, in what you
> tell me. I cannot possibly be hard upon your brother. I under-
> stand and share the wise consideration with which you regard
> his errors. With all possible respect both for Mr. Gradgrind
> and for Mr. Bounderby, I think I perceive that he has not been
> fortunate in his training. Bred at a disadvantage towards the
> society in which he has to play, he rushes into these extremes
> for himself, from opposite extremes that have long been forced
> — with the very best intentions we have no doubt — upon him.
> Mr. Bounderby's fine bluff English independence, though a
> most charming characteristic, does not — as we have agreed —
> invite confidence. If I might venture to remark that it is the
> least in the world deficient in that delicacy to which a youth
> mistaken, a character misconceived, and abilities misdirect-
> ed, would turn for relief and guidance, I should express what
> it presents to my own view.

Hypotaxis — the use of multiple subordinate clauses — dominates the
syntax, which is further complicated by parenthetical clauses such as
" — as we have agreed — ." Main clauses are delayed by preposed adjective clauses ("Bred at a disadvantage") and by suspect protestations of dif-
fidence or sincerity ("If I might venture"). Nouns are liberally modified
by adjectives, many of them evaluative and evocative of extremes
(*graceless, worldly, utmost, wise, opposite, very best,* etc.). Modals are also pro-
minent, emphasizing the speaker's claim to epistemic and deontic involvement in what he says: *cannot possibly, all possible, very best, no doubt,
most, least.* Touches of rhetoric of more identifiable origin than
Slackbridge's are present: "a youth mistaken, a character misconceived,
and abilities misdirected" is a literary, educated form associated with
writing, not oratory — the key to this literariness being the inverted structure N + Adjective (there is only one inversion, Verb + Subject, in all of
Slackbridge's speeches). Harthouse's speech in this episode is marked as
middle-class, elaborated, evasive.

At the other pole, socioeconomically and linguistically, is Stephen Blackpool. There is a detailed effort to make Stephen's language indicate his representativeness of a class. A number of different features of his language combine to make his language suggest the regional, uneducated and oral properties of the language of the Hands. He is first shown in an intimate conversation with Rachael, an introduction which makes an immediate point that his speech style is shared, not idiosyncratic. I must quote a sizeable extract, including some commentary by the narrator which offers a clear contrast of style:

"Ah, lad! 'Tis thou?" When she had said this, with a smile which would have been quite expressed, though nothing of her had been seen but her pleasant eyes, she replaced her hood again, and they went on together.

"I thought thou wast ahind me, Rachael?"

"No."

"Early t'night, lass?"

"'Times I'm a little early, Stephen; 'times a little late. I'm never to be counted on, going home."

"Nor going t'other way, neither, t'seems to me, Rachael?"

"No, Stephen."

He looked at her with some disappointment in his face, but with a respectful and patient conviction that she must be right in whatever she did. The expression was not lost upon her; she laid her hand lightly on his arm a moment, as if to thank him for it.

"We are such true friends, lad, and such old friends, and getting to be such old folk, now."

"No, Rachael, thou'rt as young as ever thou wast."

"One of us would be puzzled how to get old, Stephen, without t'other getting so too, both being alive," she answered, laughing; "but, any ways, we're such old friends, that t'hide a word of honest truth fro' one another would be a sin and a pity. 'Tis better not to walk too much together. 'Times, yes! 'Twould be hard, indeed, if 'twas not to be at all," she said, with a cheerfulness she sought to communicate to him.

"'Tis hard, anyways, Rachael."

"Try to think not; and 'twill seem better."

"I've tried a long time, and 'ta'nt got better. But thou'rt right; 'tmight make fok talk, even of thee. Thou hast been that to me, through so many year: thou hast done me so much good, and heartened of me in that cheering way, that thy word is a law to me. Ah lass, and a bright good law! Better than some real ones."

"Never fret about them, Stephen," she answered quickly, and not without an anxious glance at his face. "Let the laws be."

"Yes," he said, with a slow nod or two. "Let 'em be. Let everything be. Let all sorts alone. 'Tis a muddle, and that's aw."

A minimum of deviant spellings here serves to hint at the vowel sounds and the elisions of a northern accent. Elsewhere, Dickens indicates the accent by a more radical set of orthographic, lexical and morphological peculiarities:

"My friends," Stephen began, in the midst of a dead calm; "I ha' hed what's been spok'n o' me, and 'tis lickly that I shan't mend it. But I'd liefer you'd hearn the truth concernin myseln, fro my lips than fro onny other man's though I never cud'n speak afore so monny, wi'out bein moydert and muddled."

Detailed analyses of these dialect notations are unnecessary. Different novelists (e.g. Mrs. Gaskell, Emily Brontë) use different notational devices: some use more archaisms, others more "non-standard" morphology, and there is variation in the spelling conventions for vowels. There are two simple points to grasp in all such cases. First, these are not to be judged as realistic transcriptions where fidelity might be an issue — they are simply conventional signals of sociolinguistic difference. Second, only a very slight deviance, as in the conversation between Stephen and Rachael, is needed to persuade middle-class readers that they are in the presence of a social group below their own.

More significant is the syntax, which is in sharp contrast to Harthouse's elaborated forms. Halliday maintains that speech and writing have different information structures, and therefore different modes of syntactic organization. Writing, which can be scanned and rescanned for complexities and qualifications of meaning, is a medium which can accommodate the kinds of indirections which we noted in Harthouse's language. Speech, according to Halliday, is more straightforwardly linear, and it releases its meanings in a sequence of short chunks or "information units"; these units are segmented off by intonation patterns, rises and falls in the pitch of the voice. Syntactically, they need not be complete clauses, but are often phrases or single words, and often loosely linked by apposition or concatenation. The overall style is not strictly speaking paratactic, because the conjoined constituents are not clauses of equal weight; but in its avoidance of clause subordination it is much more like parataxis than hypotaxis.

Once the existence of this mode of speech has been pointed out, it takes no great analytic expertise to recognize that the description fits the conversation of Stephen and Rachael. The point is that Dickens has — in *writing,* of course — deliberately constructed a very *oral* model of language for these two humble characters, contrasting with the formal, written model used for some unsympathetic middle-class speakers such as Harthouse. I think there is a contrast of values intended here: solidarity and naturalness on the one hand, deviousness and insincerity on the other. I cannot prove this by reference to the language alone; I simply suggest that Dickens is using speech style stereotypes to which his readers, on the basis of their sociolinguistic competence and of their knowledge of the novel's plot, assign conventional significances.

So far I have offered examples of significant individual voices, and of speech styles which seem to take the imprint of social values ("social semiotic" in Halliday's term). Other examples could be discussed; together they would assemble a picture of a text articulated in a multitude of voices. These voices are, overall, discordant and fluc-tuating in the kaleidoscope of views they express. Furthermore, the op-posing points of view do not neatly align. Though Sleary confronts Gradgrind directly, so that the symbol of Fancy and that of Fact are in direct opposition, Harthouse and Stephen are not immediately opposed, nor many other significant antitheses of voices. Dickens's intellectual scheme for the book does not seem to have been symmetrical: his socio-linguistic symbols embodied in characters do not relate diagrammatical-ly, and so the relationships among theoretical issues such as factual edu-cation, exploitive capitalism, statistics, social reform, play, etc., are not dramatized neatly in the linguistic or narrative relationships between the characters. The story and the language figure the ideological debates in an unsettled, troubled way. I think this raggedness is a strength. But before commenting on it directly, I want to refer to other areas of linguistic instability, different from the "unpatternedness" of the global canvas. These areas involve dialogue, explicit or implicit, and figure shifting organization in the style of the voice.

Stephen Blackpool visits Bounderby's house on two occasions, and each time finds himself in a stand-up argument. The debates start with each speaker using his characteristic speech style. Bounderby is blustery and bullying, his speech packed with commands and demands:

Well Stephen, what's this I hear? What have these pests of the
earth being doing to *you?* Come in, and speak up. . . . Now,
speak up! . . . Speak up like a man.

Bounderby continues in this register (which is his constant idiolect, or a
major part of it), while Stephen's responses begin quiet and polite, in a
language heavily marked for the dialectical phonology, and based on the
short information units noticed earlier:

"What were it, sir, as yo' were pleased to want wi' me?"

"Wi' yor pardon, sir, I ha' nowt to sen about it."

"I sed as I had nowt to sen, sir; not as I was fearfo' o' openin'
my lips."

"I'm as sooary as yo, sir, when the people's leaders is bad.
They taks such as offers. Haply 'tis na' the sma'est o' their
misfortuns when they can get no better."

Pressed to state how he would solve the troubles of the weaving industry,
Stephen moves into a sequence of five long speeches; their sheer length is a
sign of departure from character, against the norm of his conversation with
Rachael. The spelling peculiarities are maintained to a large degree, as is
the syntax of spoken information; this from the third long speech:

Look round town — so rich as 'tis — and see the numbers of people as has been broughten into bein heer, fur to weave, an to
card, an to piece out a livin', aw the same one way, somehows,
twixt their cradles and their graves.

The fifth of these speeches has Stephen, under intense provocation, voic-
ing sentiments of "man" against "master" which on independent evidence,
as well as the evidence of the novel, can be associated with Dickens's own
humanitarian point of view. Stephen cannot say what will right the world,
but he can say what will not: the strong hand of the masters, *laissez-faire,*
lack of regard for the humanity of the mill-workers, and so on. When
Stephen gives voice to these sentiments, the overall structure of his
language changes to the parallelistic rhetoric of a public speech: a succession of balanced sentences, steadily increasing in length, is used to
enumerate his arguments; here are two of them:

Not drawin' nigh to fok, wi' kindness and patience an cheery
ways, that so draws nigh to one another in their monny
troubles, and so cherishes one another in their distresses wi'
what they need themseln — like, I humbly believe, as no people the genelman ha seen in aw his travels can beat — will
never do't till th' Sun turns t'ice. Most of aw, ratin 'em as so
much Power, and reg'latin 'em as if they was figures in a
soom, or machines: wi'out loves and likeins, wi'out memories
and inclinations, wi'out souls to weary and souls to
hope — when aw goes quiet, draggin on wi' 'em as if they'd
nowt o' th'kind, an when aw goes onquiet, reproachin 'e, for
their want o' sitch humanly feelins in their dealins wi' you —
this will never do't, sir, till God's work is onmade.

Some of the elaborated syntax noticed in Harthouse's language can be
found here in the internal structure of clauses, in the qualifications and
self-interruptions. And the overall format of repetitive structure recalls
the insistent harangue of the book's opening scene, in the schoolroom.

When Stephen engages with the moral issues which concern
Dickens centrally, then, his language deviates sharply from what had
earlier been offered as his own characteristic sociolinguistic style. I do
not point this out as an inconsistency of characterization, but as an application of the dialogic principle in the language through which
Stephen is constituted. The stylistic shift shows strain in Dickens's use of
a voice to express an ideological position that has become problematic
through being assigned to that speaker. Stephen as originally set up by
Dickens is inadequate to occupy the place in debate in which he has
become situated: his language strains towards the rhetoric of a more
public form of disputation than his social role warrants.

Surprising shifts of register occur in the speech of other characters,
although none so remarkable as the transformation from tongue-tied
weaver to articulate orator. I have no space to demonstrate any more of
these changes; nor, most regrettably, can I show any selection of the
range of styles of the narrative voice. Dickens ranges from subversive
parody (book 1, chap. 1, on Gradgrind on Fact), to complex animating
and de-animating metaphors (book 1, chap. 5, the superb evocation of
Coketown) to pathos, and to simple direct judgement ("He was a good
power-loom weaver, and a man of perfect integrity"). David Lodge has
analysed some varieties of the narrative rhetoric of *Hard Times* in an ex-
cellent chapter of *Language of Fiction:* analysis which readers can consult

to fill out this gap in my account. Lodge also relates these variations to uncertainties in Dickens's own position, as I do. But his judgement is essentially based on a monologic norm: "*Hard Times* succeeds where its rhetoric succeeds and fails where its rhetoric fails." Generally, Lodge argues, this rhetoric is successful when Dickens is being antagonistic or ironic, but fails when he is trying to celebrate his fictional positives.

But it is more complex than that. The various styles are not just "successful" or "failed," but transcend a two-term set of values: it is the plurality of codes, their inconstancy, and their frequent stridency, which all together constitute a fruitful and discordant polyphony. Any account of Dickens's "argument" in this novel is bound to come to the conclusion that he attacks an unmanageably large and miscellaneous range of evils (Utilitarianism in education and economics, industrial capitalism, abuse of unions, statistics, bad marriage, selfishness, etc.); that he mostly oversimplifies them (e.g. fails to see the beneficial relationship between some fact-gathering activities and real social reforms); that he is unclear on what evil causes what other evil. On the other side, his proposed palliatives are feeble, misconceived in terms of purely individual initiatives and responsibilities, and sentimentally formulated. Most of this conceptual muddle stems from the crucial inadequacy of Dickens's idealized solution of tolerant rapprochement of the two parties to the industrial situation:

> "I believe," said I, "that into the relations between employers and employed, as into all the relations of this life, there must enter something of feeling and sentiment; something of mutual explanation, forbearance, and consideration; something which is not to be found in Mr. Mc-Culloch's dictionary, and is not exactly stateable in figures; otherwise those relations are wrong and rotten at the core and will never bear sound fruit."

Translation of all Dickens's insecurely based theses and antitheses into elements and structural relationships of this novel's form has produced the asymmetries and dissonances which my stylistic analysis has begun to display. But few people today would condemn *Hard Times* as a ragged failure. The inconsistencies and discords are an indication of the problematic status of the social and theoretical crises in question for a great imagination like Dickens who could not articulate unequivocally in fiction the (unknown to him) facile solutions which were consciously available to him as theory. The novel's lack of monologic authority fits

Bakhtin's description, I believe; and the stylistic polyphony is pro-
vocative and creative, compelling the reader to grapple uneasily with
the tangle of issues that Dickens problematizes.

Deconstructing *Hard Times*

Steven Connor

Bleak House is, in obvious ways, an eminently "deconstructable" novel. Because of its very size, range and complexity, the issue of unity is a crucial one for the reader precisely because it is so difficult to achieve. The novel, we might say, is about the effort to make sense out of a mass of troublesome, diverse particulars which all the time frustrate neat and conclusive imaginative structures. Until now, literary criticism, including structuralist criticism, has concentrated on the ostensible structures of meaning in texts and has largely ignored all the hesitations, indecisions and contradictions which make up most texts and most readings of them. It is these that deconstructive criticism in part aims to restore.

But why? Why pay such obsessive attention to incoherence rather than coherence? Why not see incoherence as just an unimportant sort of interference in a text, like the crackle round a radio signal which distracts but does not prevent the signal coming through? After all, despite all this fancy talk about the text's differences from itself, don't we all mean more or less the same thing when we talk about *Bleak House?*

I think I would agree that there are dangers in allowing privileges to any kind of incoherence at the expense of any kind of coherence, for this can become just a new sort of orthodoxy. (There are signs that this is happening in some varieties of deconstructive criticism.) But it is honestly difficult to maintain that texts have the sort of coherence and intelligibility that literary criticism has been concerned to find in them. If

From *Charles Dickens.* © 1985 by Steven Connor. Basil Blackwell, 1985.

we do know more or less what we mean when we talk about *Bleak House* then that is not a function of the text itself but of the contexts, linguistic, ideological and institutional, in which we read it, all of which combine to confirm us in our recognition of *Bleak House* as a certain sort of novel. But, just as no readership can ever be wholly homogeneous — perhaps especially not the contemporary readership of 1851 — so any text is likely to be divided and inconsistent with itself in important ways. If meaning is dependent upon differences in language, then those differences are likely to split and differentiate meaning itself.

All this doesn't mean, however, a licence to mash any text up into a dog's breakfast, about which anyone can say more or less what they like. On the contrary, deconstructive criticism sets out to try to show the particular ways in which the conflict between presence and difference is established in texts, and in which the awareness of the conflict is then repressed. One of the clearest formulations of this I know is Barbara Johnson's:

> *Deconstruction* is not synonymous with *destruction*. . . . The deconstruction of a text does not proceed by random doubt or arbitrary subversion, but by the careful teasing out of warring forces of signification within the text itself. If anything is destroyed in a deconstructive reading, it is not the text, but the claim to unequivocal domination of one mode of signifying over another. A deconstructive reading is a reading that analyzes the specificity of a text's critical difference from itself.
>
> (*The Critical Difference: Essays in the Contemporary Rhetoric of Reading*)

It is because of this that Dickens's later novels seem to offer themselves for deconstructive criticism, even, in a sense, to deconstruct themselves from within; as the novels project increasingly complex and contradictory fictional worlds, the desire to enclose and control those worlds grows in proportion to the intensity of the internal arguments that the novels conduct with themselves.

There is, however, one novel of this period in which, most critics are agreed, there is not quite the same conflict between coherence and incoherence. That novel is *Hard Times*. Many readers of the novel have been disappointed by the way that the issues with which it deals seem to have been conclusively sewn up from the start. The insistence with which it seems to present its rigid binary opposition between "system" and "fact," exemplified in Gradgrind's school and Bounderby's mill, and "life" and "fancy," exemplified in Sleary's circus, has seemed to many readers to make *Hard Times* seem more like a diagram or fable than a proper novel, pulsating with complex human life. John Lucas articulates this view when he writes [in *The Melancholy Man*] that "*Hard Times* is in the grip of an idea" and this view seems to be shared by different critics employing different methodologies.

This would seem to make *Hard Times* a good test case for a deconstructive analysis like the one I have just described. What can deconstruction do with such a simple and reductive text, one that seems to have done so complete a job of silencing all internal dissension?

One way to approach this would be to look at the ways in which the principal thematic issues are represented in linguistic terms in the text, in order to examine the way in which the text's own form and language represent its content. As with *Bleak House*, metaphor and metonymy provide a good starting-point.

From the first pages of the novel it is clear that Gradgrindery is to be characterized by an excess of metaphor, shown in the desire for absolute interchangeability between signifiers and signifieds. The definition of a horse that Bitzer offers relies upon the implicit claim that language can account absolutely for the things it names, so that, having heard the definition, Sissy is expected immediately to "know what a horse is" (book 1, chap. 2). In Gradgrindery, the assumption is that, because signs can substitute absolutely for things, they are indistinguishable from them—therefore, since horses do not walk up and down walls in reality, you should not paper walls with representations of horses, and, since you don't walk over flowers in reality (an odd assumption, this, for Gradgrind), you shouldn't put representations of flowers in a carpet. Gradgrind's rage for substitution means that he can conceive easily of perfect translations of one sign into another—"'What is called Taste, is only another name for Fact'"(book 1, chap. 2).

Sissy Jupe, however, has a different view of representation, recognizing that the difference between the reality and the representation means that you can't hurt a picture of a flower. For Gradgrind, no such distinction between signifier and signified exists, and especially not in speaking of himself, where his words correspond exactly with his image of what he is:

> In such terms Mr Gradgrind always mentally introduced himself, whether to his private circle of acquaintance, or to the public in general. In such terms, no doubt, substituting the words "boys and girls," for "Sir," Thomas Gradgrind now

presented Thomas Gradgrind to the little pitchers before him
who were to be filled so full of facts.

(BOOK I, CHAP. 2)

The image which recurs throughout the book to designate this
perfect equivalence is the mathematical calculation; Gradgrind sees
himself as "a man who proceeds upon the principle that two and two are
four, and nothing over, and who is not to be talked into allowing for
anything over" (book 1, chap. 2). This mode of exact substitution is
characteristic not only of Gradgrind but of the other Utilitarian
characters in the book. Bounderby announces his linguistic creed in his
wedding speech:

> "as you all know me, and know what I am, and what my ex-
> traction was, you won't expect a speech from a man who, when
> he sees a Post, says, 'that's a Post,' and when he sees a Pump,
> says, 'that's a Pump,' and is not to be got to call a Post a Pump,
> or a Pump a Post, or either of them a Toothpick."

(BOOK I, CHAP. 16)

Bounderby is surrounded by objects in the material world which
act as perfect signifiers for him; the correspondence between him and his
front door is an absolute one:

> [Bounderby] lived, in a red house with black outside shutters,
> green inside blinds, a black street door, up two white steps,
> BOUNDERBY (in letters very like himself) upon a brazen
> plate, and a round brazen door-handle underneath it, like a
> brazen full-stop.

(BOOK I, CHAP. 12)

Dickens's description here turns metonymy, the separate, con-
tiguous details of Bounderby's house and front door, into metaphor,
since every detail is merely a repetition of the designation "BOUNDER-
BY." The figure is therefore that "metaphoricized metonymy" which we
have seen operating before (see discussion of *Dombey and Son* [in *Charles
Dickens*]). This kind of figurative exchange is found in descriptions of the
Coketown workers, too:

> In the hardest working part of Coketown . . . where the
> chimneys, for want of air to make a draught, were built in an
> immense variety of stunted and crooked shapes as though

every house put out a sign of the kind of people who might be expected to be born in it; among the multitude of Coketown, generically called "the Hands,"—a race who would have found more favour with some people, if Providence had seen fit to make them only hands, or, like the lower creatures of the seashore, only hands and stomachs—lived a certain Stephen Blackpool, forty years of age.

(BOOK I, CHAP. 10)

The "stunted and crooked shapes" are here not metonymic details connoting variety and difference, but metaphoric signs, like Bounderby's front door, which signify only an identical poverty. The remarks about the "hands" remind us that the narrowing of metonymy into metaphorical substitution (for all functional purposes, the men and women consist only of their hands), is an actual violence as well as a quirk of language.

As we might expect, the contrasting world of Fancy in the novel is characterized by a different attitude towards language and representation, and evoked in the text by different figurative means. Where Gradgrind's world is one of metaphorical substitution, the world of Fancy is characterized by metonymic accretion. This is brought out very well in the description of the sign outside the Pegasus's Arms:

The name of the public house was the Pegasus's Arms. The Pegasus's legs might have been more to the purpose; but, underneath the winged horse upon the sign-board, The Pegasus's Arms was inscribed in Roman letters. Beneath that inscription again, in a flowing scroll, the painter had touched off the lines:

> Good malt makes good beer,
> Walk in, and they'll draw it here;
> Good wine makes good brandy,
> Give us a call and you'll find it handy.

Framed and glazed upon the wall behind the dingy little bar, was another Pegasus—a theatrical one— with real gauze let in for his wings, golden stars stuck on all over him, and his ethereal harness made of red silk.

(BOOK I, CHAP. 6)

Obviously the sign of the bar does correspond metaphorically in some respects with Sleary's circus, in its fantastic improvisation of detail and its good-humoured dinginess. But what is more noticeable about the sign and the description of it is the way that this simple kind of reading of correspondence is deflected and postponed. The signboard is, in fact, a series of metonymies, moving through the arms, legs and wings of Pegasus, the inscriptions beneath the picture, and into the details of the framed and glazed Pegasus inside the bar, with an energy that makes it difficult to see the bar sign as stable and self-contained. The discontinuity of signifier and signified is also brought about by the close attention to signifiers themselves, in their material shape and texture, the "Roman letters" and "flowing scroll" of the inscriptions and the gauze and silk of the framed Pegasus, as well as by the splitting of the signboard into three signifiers — the painting of Pegasus, the inscription beneath which names it (and the bar, of course) and the verse beneath that inscription, each new signifier making a signified of the previous signifier. The sign therefore creatively exceeds what it signifies, in a way that contrasts very markedly with Bounderby's front door; the sign and the description of it produce a metonymic deferral rather than a metaphoric fixing of Sleary's circus.

This is reinforced by the inefficiency and indistinctness of language itself in Sleary's world. The circus people's manner of speaking, with its private slang (outlandish to Gradgrind's ears), seems to emphasize the resistant material quality of language, rather than the communication of specific meanings. Sleary's heavy, bronchial speech does the same thing and reminds the reader incidentally of the "corpulent slow boy, with a wheezy manner of breathing" who mistakes Gradgrind's intentions in the classroom and offers free association instead of reasoning (book 1, chap. 2).

The opposition of Fact and Fancy in *Hard Times* also results in a structured contrast between different kinds of and attitudes towards fiction. Where Gradgrind is suspicious of any fiction which exceeds verifiable fact, Fancy expresses itself indomitably in fictional forms which transgress the rules of realism or plausibility. It is for this reason that fairy tale is so important in *Hard Times* (as in many other Dickens novels); fairy tale is precisely that form of narrative which permits imaginative exceeding of the limits of the real world. It is appropriate that the story that Sissy remembers telling her father should be that of Scheherezade, in which a princess staves off her execution by telling a succession of stories; it is a narrative which is actually about the deferment of reality by an excess of narrative. But even realistic fiction, "about men and women, more or less like themselves, and about children, more or less like their own" is regarded by the Coketown workers as a sort of relaxing addition to their lives, rather than an inert reflection of them, and Gradgrind is perplexed "at this eccentric sum, and he never could make out how it yielded this unaccountable product" (book 1, chap. 8).

So we can see that, as in *Bleak House,* the opposition between different kinds of language and different attitudes towards it is a way of sustaining important thematic oppositions in the book. As in *Bleak House,* the contrast seems to be between metaphor and metonymy, or language as presence and language as difference. We ought to pause here, however, to notice an interesting reversal. In *Bleak House,* we remember, it is the metaphorical world of Jarndyce and Esther which the narrative accredits against the endlessly multiplying, metonymic confusion of Chancery and the public world. But in *Hard Times* metaphor, or language as presence, stands condemned as characteristic of the life-denying world of Gradgrindery, while metonymy and difference are the guarantees of life, communication and "amuthement."

This is not to say that these distinctions are maintained absolutely. We saw [elsewhere] how, in *Bleak House,* they were liable to be inverted in important ways, and the same seems to be true of *Hard Times.* Gradgrind's ruthless commitment to the public world of fact often manifests itself in a wasteful surplus of written material which is reminiscent of Chancery, as in the endless pamphlets that he produces on social questions — "little rivers of tabular statements periodically flowed into the howling ocean of tabular statements, which no diver ever got to any depth in and came up sane" (book 1, chap. 8). Opposed to this is the dignity and rugged earnestness of Stephen's speech (book 2, chap. 4) and the primarily oral culture of the mill-workers — one of the principal grounds of objection to Slackbridge is the elaborately "written" quality of his language, with its effacement of dialect and suspicious complexity of syntax.

These inconsistencies indicate the arbitrariness of the contrasts which are set up in the novel and therefore in some ways threaten its thematic unity. Even more interesting and problematic is the way that Dickens's own language, produced as it necessarily is between the axes of the metaphorical and metonymic, is involved in this opposition and inversion of opposition.

The first thing to strike us ought to be the very high degree of metaphoric substitution in Dickens's own language. Much of this is evidently ironical, as in the description of Bounderby's front door or of the schoolroom in the opening paragraphs of the novel:

The scene was a plain, bare, monotonous vault of a
schoolroom, and the speaker's square forefinger emphasized
his observations by underscoring every sentence with a line
on the schoolmaster's sleeve. The emphasis was helped by the
speaker's square wall of a forehead, which had his eyebrows
for its base, while his eyes found commodious cellarage in two
dark caves, overshadowed by the wall.

(BOOK I, CHAP. I)

The speaker and the schoolmaster are here shrunk down to particular attributes, forefinger, sleeve, forehead, eyebrows and eyes,
which then come to stand as complete images of them. This is again the
metaphoricized metonymy found at the begining of *Dombey and Son* and
it gives something of the same sense of premature closure. But here there
seems to be even less room for invention and free ranging over detail;
even the metonymical relationship between the speaker and his sur-
roundings is forced grimly into a relationship of metaphorical exchange,
with the similarity between the "plain, bare" schoolroom and the
speaker's "square wall of a forehead" and the connection between the
"monotonous vault" of the room and the "two dark caves" of his eyes. In
this passage, the text inflicts the same violent reduction on Gradgrind as
he inflicts upon the world.

The irony is clear here, the very niggardliness of the narration
marks it as an imitation of Gradgrind's putative style rather than the
authentic voice of the narrator — if Gradgrind were writing a novel, it
seems to say, this is the kind of parched and grudging stuff he would produce. The limitations of excessive reliance on metaphorical substitution
are therefore asserted by implication and a longing for the liberating
openness of metonymy established.

The interesting thing is that Dickens's narrative only rarely satisfies
this longing. Metaphorical modes appear insistently throughout the
narrative and often in much less ironic ways. In a sense, the whole purpose of the novel is to convince us of a number of equivalences, most
particularly that between the educational philosophy of Gradgrind and
the economic theory and practice of the new industrialism; and it is in
metaphor that this association is established. The descriptions of
Gradgrind and Bounderby in book 1, chapters 1 and 4 establish a number
of similarities between them which assist the metaphorical transposition of
their roles and social positions: both men are more inanimate than
animate, Gradgrind being like a wall, and Bounderby being "brassy";

both have distorted shapes, though in different ways—Gradgrind is recurrently "square" while Bounderby is round, "puffed," "swelled" and "inflated" and both have bullying postures. One particular metaphor is applied to both of them in a way that seals the resemblance; Gradgrind's hair is described as "a plantation of firs to keep the wind from its shining surface" (book 1, chap. 1), while Bounderby's hair is "all standing up in disorder . . . in that condition from being constantly blown about by his windy boastfulness" (book 1, chap. 4). The equivalence between Gradgrind and Bounderby makes the interchangeability of industry and education upon which Dickens insists seem natural and solid (though also, of course, to be condemned).

It may seem rather odd that when, on one level, the novel is a condemnation of the metaphorical or substitutive frame of mind, Dickens should resort to metaphor to affirm the structural resemblances in his novel. Another example of the way that *Hard Times* connives in what it condemns is the account given of the predatory voyeurism of Mrs Sparsit as she spies on Louisa and Harthouse. Her fixation expresses itself in a metaphor:

> Now, Mrs Sparsit was not a poetical woman; but she took an idea in the nature of an allegorical fancy, into her head. . . . She erected in her mind a mighty Staircase, with a dark pit of shame and ruin at the bottom; and down those stairs, from day to day and hour to hour, she saw Louisa coming.
>
> (BOOK 2, CHAP. 10)

Mrs Sparsit's obsession with this metaphor is extreme and is clearly a mark of her jealous attempts to control and exploit people and events. The metaphor is of course a highly melodramatic one, and there is something satisfyingly appropriate about Mrs Sparsit's unconscious choice of this debased literary mode to embody her spite. But, although Dickens's narrative distances itself from the metaphor by means of its irony, it also begins to adopt it for itself and to extract profit from it. The Staircase becomes Dickens's leitmotiv as well as Mrs Sparsit's *idée fixe*—"The figure descended the great stairs, steadily, steadily; always verging, like a weight in deep water, to the black gulf at the bottom . . . . Very near bottom now. Upon the brink of the abyss . . . She elopes! She falls from the lowermost stair, and is swallowed up in the gulf!" (book 2, chap. 10). The titles of the chapters, "Lower and Lower" and "Down" also emphasize the theft of the image, as does the culminating scene of book 2, in which Louisa, having reached the bottom of the descent, falls in an insensible heap at her father's feet.

The unconscious complicity between Dickens's language and Mrs Sparsit's is a sign of a more deeply rooted association between the dominant metaphorical mode of signification in Dickens's text and the metaphorical mode of signification it condemns in Gradgrind and the party of Fact. Metaphor is repeatedly used to discredit metaphor as Dickens mounts a systematic assault on systematic thought.

All this is despite the fact that Dickens's own narrative tries repeatedly to associate itself with the fanciful openness of fairy tale. Often fairy-tale images and references seem to offer an ironic kind of compensation for or revenge on the narrative and linguistic failure of the masters of Coketown, as, for example, when Gradgrind's room is compared to Bluebeard's chamber (book 1, chap. 15), or when Mrs Sparsit is described (absurdly) as the Bank Fairy and (more acceptably) as the Bank Dragon (book 2, chap. 1). We've seen how fairy tale is presented in *Hard Times* as a metonymic mode, typified by excess and casual association of ideas. Certainly, some of these authorial references to fairy tale have this playfulness about them, as with the running joke about the mills being "fairy palaces" with their "melancholy-mad elephants." But fairy tale is often used in another way, to fix, caricature and punish — as, for example, in the repeated characterization of Mrs Sparsit as a witch. The allusion to Ali Baba and the Forty Thieves which ends the second chapter does this, too; there is a show of whimsicality in the way that the details of the correspondence are improvised, but the concluding metaphor actually locks together the two halves of the equivalence in a way that narrows and fixes the reader's understanding rather than releasing it:

> He went to work in this preparatory lesson, not unlike Morgiana in the Forty Thieves: looking into all the vessels ranged before him, one after another, to see what they contained. Say, good M'Choakumchild . . . When from thy boiling store, thou shalt fill each jar brim full by-and-by, dost thou think that thou wilt always kill outright the robber Fancy lurking within — or sometimes only maim him and distort him!
>
> (BOOK I, CHAP. 2)

Dickens's narrative here takes possession of the idea of fairy tale in a way that shows surprisingly how apt the simplification of character and situation of fairy tale is to express the caricaturing outlook of Gradgrindery. This association is made even more firmly a couple of chapters later when a nursery rhyme is used to sum up the dismissive attitude of officialdom to the Coketown workers:

There was an old woman, and what do you think?
She lived upon nothing but victuals and drink;
Victuals and drink were the whole of her diet,
And yet this old woman would NEVER be quiet.

(BOOK I. CHAP. 5)

Clearly the use of the nursery rhyme is a deliberate insult to the dignity of Gradgrind and Bounderby, at the same time as it is a parody of their insulting attitude toward the Coketown workers and thus a device to focus the scorn of reader and author alike. But the status of the nursery rhyme is interestingly ambivalent here; does it stand as an example of liberating fancy, or as a characterization of the brutalizing simplications of the Utilitarian outlook?

These examples of inconsistency in the use of metaphor and metonymy may not strike us in themselves as conclusive proof of the novel's self-deconstruction, but they do reflect an uncertainty about language, and particularly about the kind of language to be used in representing such strict binary oppositions as the one between Fact and Fancy. It comes down to a matter of authority. The text of *Hard Times* relies upon a notion of presence, upon its contract with its readers that it is speaking of real people and events, that its signifiers substitute for real signifieds, in order to give authority to its recommendation of the metonymic openness of Fancy. But if taken seriously the accreditation of metonymy and difference will tend to undo the firm opposition of Fact and Fancy essential to the book. The text is therefore recommending an openness of interpretation which it must itself resist in order that the recommendation may be made in the first place. Or, to put it another way, the text has to be strictly systematic in order to construct its condemnation of system.

The paradox produces some moments of uneasiness in the novel, not least in the rather odd relationship between seriousness and levity which it displays. The text recommends "amuthement" against the dogged earnestness of Gradgrindery, but itself lacks the expansive and anarchic comedy, and particularly the comically self-conscious use of language which characterizes other novels. The uncertainty about verbal comedy and its implications is made clear interestingly at the moment when Sissy makes a mistake in telling Louisa about her performance at school:

"Then Mr M'Choakumchild said he would try me once more. And he said, Here are the stutterings—"

"Statistics," said Louisa.

"Yes, Miss Louisa—they always remind me of stutterings, and that's another of my mistakes."

(BOOK I, CHAP. 9)

There is a neat little joke here and it's a pity to be tedious about it, but I think it is worth spelling out what is going on. The joke involves, of course, the opposition between the ideas of efficiency and inefficiency in language. The word "stutterings" is obviously in one sense mere noise, whose only meaning consists in representing Sissy's difficulty in pronouncing the word "statistics." This kind of inefficiency of language is not without its own significance in *Hard Times,* as we have seen, for it associates Sissy with the metonymic openness of the language of Sleary and the circus. Sissy's stuttering corresponds to Sleary's lisp, for both bring forward the materiality of signifiers, which delays or prevents the simple substitution of words for things. Indeed, Sissy's own name is involved in this. "Cecilia" probably gives Sleary as much difficulty in pronunciation as "statistics" gives Sissy, and, of course, as far as Gradgrind is concerned, "Sissy" represents just the same objectionable metonymic slide away from distinctness as the use of "stutterings" for "statistics" (Sleary's own name seems to include a slide between "slurring" and "blearing").

But of course the joke consists in the happy accident that "stutterings" is, not just a meaningless mistake. The word that Sissy hits upon *does* have meaning, in that it is an implied judgement on the inefficiency of statistics themselves. Useless as they are for the measurement and understanding of the subtleties of human feeling, statistics really are just "stutterings." It is therefore crucial to the joke that "stutterings" should be meaningless and meaningful at the same time—it would hardly work as well if Sissy thought of "stilts" or "stalactites." But this brings about an inversion in the sign. The inefficient metonymy becomes an efficient, meaningful metaphor, while the metaphor ("statistics") becomes mere sound, as inefficient as we have taken Sissy's mistake to be.

This inversion involves other factors too. For one thing, it inverts the relationship between adult and child. The authoritative world is shown to be really only as playful and silly as the fanciful world of children. The joke plays as well on the opposition of speech and writing, for the authority of the written mode of statistics is undone by the oral mistake that Sissy makes. We could project some of the swapping of places which takes place in the joke into a diagram (the horizontal lines indicate the original associations, the diagonal lines the new associations established by the joke):

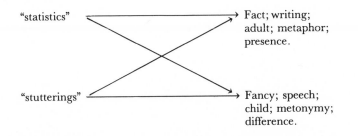

"statistics" → Fact; writing; adult; metaphor; presence.

"stutterings" → Fancy; speech; child; metonymy; difference.

But this brings about an instability or "stutter" in Dickens's own narration and in the reader's reception of it. Sissy's innocent use of the word and the narrative's knowing use of it are incompatible with each other, though, because of the structure of the joke, they are also necessary to each other. The reader therefore flickers between the two readings, the adult and the childish, the meaningful and the meaningless, without being able to decide which has priority. The joke has a residue of internal difference which makes it difficult to decide on a serious or nonserious reading. Most importantly, it represents the deconstruction of the narrative's claim to authoritative language, because the joke reveals the structure of difference which constitutes authority of meaning.

Perhaps the most striking example of the dispersal of meaning is to be found in the language of Mrs Gradgrind. Though she is in many ways just a victim of the dominion of Fact, her scattered wits and language also associate her with the world of Fancy in the novel. For, in some senses, her feebleness with language is a strength; her vagueness about names, for example, and, in particular, her inability to use Bounderby's name after he marries Louisa, is a comic resistance to the rage for permanence of naming.

But there is also something very frightening about the tenuous grasp of language which Mrs Gradgrind has. Her subservience to a language which, instead of being her instrument, seems to speak uncontrollably through her, is like that of many characters in *Bleak House;* like the victims of Chancery, Mrs Gradgrind feels that she "never hears the last of anything," because there is no end to language as difference. Personal identity is difficult to pin down once it is divided in this way by language, so that Mrs Gradgrind cannot even be sure that the pain she feels is her own. She ends up fixated upon an obscure and unnameable sense of lack:

"there is something—not an Ology at all—that your father has missed, or forgotten, Louisa. I don't know what it is. I have often sat with Sissy near me, and thought about it. I shall never get its name now. But your father may. It makes me restless. I want to write to him, to find out for God's sake, what it is. Give me a pen, give me a pen.

(BOOK 2, CHAP. 9)

Something strange has happened here; the metonymic diffusion of Fancy has come to seem like a symptom of the alienated language of Fact. It is as though the dominating structure of *Hard Times* had turned into that of *Bleak House*. The language of Mrs Gradgrind, both in her distracted speech, and in the "figures of wonderful no-meaning" she traces with her imaginary pen, poses a challenge to the stability and coherence of *Hard Times*. She represents the largest of a number of blind spots in the novel where the dispersing play of language as difference is activated. The narrative officially celebrates but implicitly condemns and therefore represses this play of difference; but its very meaning is in a sense built upon it.

It is in the nature of these internal arguments within texts to be inconclusive. I have not been trying to build a case that, unknown to so many readers for so many years, *Hard Times* is really a gloriously fragmented modernist or post-modernist text which flaunts its incoherence and demands that its reader join in the vandalism of all meaning. What I do find interesting in the novel is the way that our firm convictions of the clarity of its structure actually require the suspension of awareness of certain rather important internal inconsistencies. These inconsistencies have a residual force though, working athwart the main narrative but also, in a peculiar way, sustaining it.

This is to say, then, that if our sense of the coherence and structural simplicity of *Hard Times* is an illusion, then it is a necessary illusion. Reading is a continually renewed struggle between the openness of text and the satisfying closure of interpretation. Each is related to the other indissolubly. Seen in this way, *Hard Times* may come to seem a little less naive. Because the book is so committed to the projection of the stark opposites of Fact and Fancy, the risk is all the greater of discovering it to be haunted by internal difference, of the book being revealed as another text entirely from the one it represents itself to be. Nevertheless, this is the dangerous story that *Hard Times* begins to tell about itself.

This is not the last account that Dickens attempts to give of the conflict between "humanity" and "system." . . . [T]he problematic shiftings between metaphor and metonymy, presence and difference, are more than just linguistic issues; they are related to fundamental questions about the nature and formation of identity in society and to specific questions of authority and power.

Chronology

1812   Charles John Huffam Dickens, the second of eight children, born February 7 to John and Elizabeth Dickens.

1814   John Dickens, a clerk in the Navy Pay Office, is transferred from Portsea to London. During these early years, from 1814 to 1821, Dickens is taught his letters by his mother, and he immerses himself in the fiction classics of his father's library.

1817   John Dickens moves family to Chatham.

1821   Dickens begins school with the son of a Baptist minister; he remains at this school for a time even after his family is transferred again to London in 1822.

1824   John Dickens is arrested for debt and sent to Marshalsea Prison, accompanied by his wife and younger children. Charles soon finds lodging in a poor neighborhood and begins work at Warren's Blacking Factory. His father is released three months later and Charles returns to school.

1824–26   Dickens attends Wellington House Academy, London.

1827   Works as a law clerk and spends time reading in the British Museum.

1830   Meets Maria Beadnell; he eventually falls in love with her, but she jilts him upon return from a trip to Paris in 1833.

1831   Becomes a reporter for the *Mirror of Parliament*.

1832   Becomes a staff writer for the *True Sun*.

1833   Dickens's first published piece, "A Dinner at Poplar Walk," appears in December issue of the *Monthly Magazine* under the pen name "Boz."

1834   Dickens becomes a staff writer on the *Morning Chronicle*. His "street sketches" begin to appear in the *Evening Chronicle*. Dickens meets his future wife, Catherine Hogarth. Also, John Dickens is arrested again for debt.

1836   *Sketches by Boz,* illustrated by George Cruikshank, published. Dickens marries Catherine Hogarth in April. Also in this year, his first play, *The Strange Gentleman,* runs for two months at the St. James's Theatre. A second play, *The Village Coquettes,* is produced at the same theater. Dickens meets John Forster, who becomes a lifelong friend and his biographer.

1836–37   *Pickwick Papers* published in monthly installments from April through the following November.

1837   *Pickwick Papers* appears in book form. *Oliver Twist* begins to appear in *Bentley's Miscellany. Is She His Wife?* produced at the St. James's. Dickens's first child born, and the family moves to Doughty Street. Catherine's sister Mary, deeply loved by Dickens, dies suddenly.

1838   *Nicholas Nickleby* appears in installments; completed in October of 1839. Dickens's first daughter born.

1839   The Dickenses move to Devonshire Terrace. A second daughter born. *Nickleby* appears in book form.

1840   Dickens edits *Master Humphrey's Clock,* a weekly periodical, in which *The Old Curiosity Shop* appears.

1841   *Barnaby Rudge* appears in *Master Humphrey's Clock.* Another son born.

1842   Dickens and his wife tour America from January to June; Dickens publishes *American Notes* and begins *Martin Chuzzlewit.*

1843   *Martin Chuzzlewit* appears in monthly installments (January 1843–July 1844). *A Christmas Carol* published.

1844   Dickens tours Italy and Switzerland. Another Christmas book, *The Chimes,* completed. A third son born.

1845   Dickens produces *Every Man in his Humour* in England. *The Cricket on the Hearth* is written by Christmas, and Dickens begins *Pictures from Italy.* A fourth son born.

1846   Dickens creates and edits the *Daily News,* but resigns as editor after seventeen days. Begins *Dombey and Son* while in Lausanne; the novel appears in twenty monthly installments (October 1846–April 1848). *The Battle of Life: A Love Story* appears for Christmas.

1847   Dickens begins to manage a theatrical company and arranges a benefit tour of *Every Man in his Humour.* Fifth son born.

1848   Daughter Fanny dies. Dickens's theatrical company performs for Queen Victoria. It also performs *The Merry Wives of Windsor* to raise money for the preservation of Shakespeare's birthplace. Dickens's last Christmas book, *The Haunted Man,* published.

1849   Dickens begins *David Copperfield* (published May 1849–November 1850). A sixth son born.

1850   *Household Words,* a weekly periodical, established with Dickens as editor. A third daughter born, who dies within a year.

1851   Dickens and his company participate in theatrical fundraising. Dickens's father dies.

1852   *Bleak House* appears in monthly installments (March 1852 – September 1853). The first bound volume of *A Child's History of England* appears. Dickens's last child, his seventh son, born.

1853   Dickens gives first public readings, from the Christmas books. Travels to France and Italy.

1854   *Hard Times* published in *Household Words* (April 1–August 12) and appears in book form.

1855   *Little Dorrit* appears in monthly installments (December 1855–June 1857). Dickens and family travel at year's end to Paris, where the novelist meets other leading literary and theatrical persons.

1856   Dickens purchases Gad's Hill Place, and the family returns to London.

1857   Dickens is involved primarily with theatrical productions.

1858   Dickens announces his separation from his wife, about which he writes a personal statement in *Household Words.*

1859   Dickens concludes *Household Words* and establishes a new weekly, *All the Year Round. A Tale of Two Cities* appears there from April 20 to November 26, and is published in book form in December.

1860   *Great Expectations* underway in weekly installments (December 1860 – August 1861).

1861   *The Uncommercial Traveller,* a collection of pieces from *All the Year Round,* published.

1862   Dickens gives many public readings and travels to Paris.

1863   Dickens continues his readings in Paris and London.

Daughter Elizabeth dies.

1864   *Our Mutual Friend* appears in monthly installments for publisher Chapman and Hall (May 1864–November 1865).

1865   Dickens suffers a stroke that leaves him lame. Involved in train accident, which causes him to change the ending of *Our Mutual Friend*. *Our Mutual Friend* appears in book form. The second collection of *The Uncommercial Traveller* published.

1866   Dickens gives thirty public readings in the English provinces.

1867   Continues the provincial readings, then travels to America in November, where he reads in Boston and New York. This tour permanently breaks the novelist's health.

1868   In April, Dickens returns to England, where he continues to tour.

1869   The first public reading of the murder of Nancy (from *Oliver Twist*) performed, but his doctors recommend he discontinue the tour. *The Mystery of Edwin Drood* begun.

1870   Dickens gives twelve readings in London. Six parts of *Edwin Drood* appear from April to September. On June 9, Charles Dickens dies, aged 58. He is buried in the Poets' Corner, Westminster Abbey.

Contributors

HAROLD BLOOM, Sterling Professor of the Humanities at Yale University, is the author of *The Anxiety of Influence, Poetry and Repression,* and many other volumes of literary criticism. His forthcoming study, *Freud: Transference and Authority*, attempts a full-scale reading of all of Freud's major writings. A MacArthur Prize Fellow, he is general editor of five series of literary criticism published by Chelsea House.

RAYMOND WILLIAMS, Judith F. Wilson Professor of Drama at Cambridge University, is the most influential of British Marxist critics of literature. His books include *Culture and Society, The Long Revolution,* and *The Country and the City.*

ROBERT E. LOUGY is Professor of English at Pennsylvania State University. His publications include studies of Dickens, Thackeray, Swinburne, and nineteenth-century poetics. The author of *Charles Robert Maturin,* he has recently edited *The Children and the Chapel.*

ROBERT BARNARD is the author of *Imagery and Theme in the Novels of Dickens,* as well as many mystery novels.

GEOFFREY THURLEY's books include *The Dickens Myth: Its Genesis and Structure, The Turbulent Dream: Passion and Politics in the Poetry of W. B. Yeats, The Romantic Predicament,* and *Counter-Modernism in Current Critical Theory.*

JOSEPH BUTWIN is Professor of English at the University of Washington. He is coauthor, with Frances Butwin, of *Sholom Aleichem,* and has written on nineteenth-century political satire.

PETER BRACHER is Professor of English at Wright State University. A Dickens specialist, he has written several studies of Dickens's early publishing history and reception, as well as articles on the Bible, literature, and public education.

133

Roger Fowler is the Dean of English and American Studies at the University of East Anglia. He is the author of *Introduction to Transformational Syntax, Linguistics and the Novel,* and *Literature as Social Discourse: The Practice of Linguistic Criticism.*

Steven Connor is Lecturer in English at Birbeck College in London. He is the author of *Charles Dickens.*

Bibliography

Baird, John D. "'Divorce and Matrimonial Causes': An Aspect of *Hard Times.*" *Victorian Studies* 20 (1977): 401–12.

Bornstein, George. "Miscultivated Field and Corrupted Garden: Imagery in *Hard Times.*" *Nineteenth-Century Fiction* 26 (1971): 158–70.

Collins, Philip, ed. *Dickens: The Critical Heritage.* New York: Barnes & Noble, 1971.

Deneau, Daniel P. "The Brother-Sister Relationship in *Hard Times.*" *Dickensiana* 60, no. 3 (1964): 173–77.

Dyson, A. E. *The Inimitable Dickens: A Reading of the Novels.* New York: St. Martin's, 1970.

Engel, Monroe. *The Maturity of Dickens.* Cambridge: Harvard University Press, 1958.

Fielding, K. J., and Harriet Martineau. "*Hard Times* and the Factory Controversy." In *Dickens Centennial Essays,* edited by Ada Nisbet and Blake Nevius, 22–45. Berkeley: University of California Press, 1971.

Ford, George, and Sylvère Monod, eds. *Charles Dickens:* Hard Times. A Norton Critical Edition. New York: Norton, 1966.

Forster, John. *The Life of Charles Dickens.* Edited by A. J. Hoppe. 2 vols. London: J. M. Dent, 1966.

Gibson, John W. "*Hard Times:* A Further Note." *Dickens Studies* 1, no. 2 (1965): 90–101.

Gold, Joseph. "'Aw a Muddle': *Hard Times.*" In *Charles Dickens: Radical Moralist,* 196–207. Minneapolis: University of Minnesota Press, 1972.

Goldberg, Michael. "The Critique of Utility: *Hard Times.*" In *Carlyle and Dickens,* 78–99. Athens: University of Georgia Press, 1972.

Gray, Paul Edward, ed. *Twentieth Century Interpretations of* Hard Times: *A Collection of Critical Essays.* Englewood Cliffs, N. J.: Prentice-Hall, 1969.

Haberman, Melvyn. "The Courtship of the Void: The World of *Hard Times.*" In *The Worlds of Victorian Fiction,* edited by Jerome H. Buckley, 37–56. Cambridge: Harvard University Press, 1975.

Hirsch, David M. "*Hard Times* and Dr. Leavis." *Criticism* 6 (Winter 1964): 1–16.

Hollington, Michael. "Ironic Infernos: *Bleak House, Hard Times,* and Ruskin's Conception of the Grotesque." In *Dickens and the Grotesque,* 192–215. Totowa, N. J.: Barnes & Noble, 1984.

Holloway, John. "*Hard Times:* A History and a Criticism." In *Dickens and the Twentieth Century,* edited by John Gross and Gabriel Pearson, 159–74. Toronto: University of Toronto Press, 1962.

Horne, Lewis B. "Hope and Memory in *Hard Times.*" *The Dickensian* 75, no. 389 (1979): 167–73.

House, Humphrey. *The Dickens World.* 2d ed. London: Oxford University Press, 1961.

House, Madeleine, et al., eds. *The Letters of Charles Dickens.* Pilgrim Edition. New York: Oxford University Press, 1965–.

Johnson, Alan P. "*Hard Times:* 'Performance' or 'Poetry'?" *Dickens Studies* 5 (1969): 62–80.

Larson, Janet Karsten. "Identity's Fictions: Naming and Renaming in *Hard Times.*" *Dickens Studies Newsletter* 10, no. 1 (1979): 14–19.

Leavis, F. R. *The Great Tradition.* New York: New York University Press, 1963.

Leavis, F. R., and Q. D. Leavis. *Dickens the Novelist.* London: Chatto & Windus, 1970.

Linehan, Thomas M. "Rhetorical Technique and Moral Purpose in *Hard Times.*" *University of Toronto Quarterly* 47, no. 1 (1977): 22–36.

Lodge, David. *Language of Fiction: Essays in Criticism and Verbal Analysis of the English Novel.* New York: Columbia University Press, 1966.

McGillis, Roderick F. "Plum Pies and Factories: Cross Connections in *Hard Times.*" *Dickens Studies Newsletter* 11, no. 4 (1980): 102–7.

Mackenzie, Norman, and Jeanne Mackenzie. *Dickens: A Life.* New York: Oxford University Press, 1979.

Monod, Sylvère. "*Hard Times:* An Undickensian Novel?" In *Studies in the Later Dickens,* edited by Jean-Claude Amalric, 71–92. Montpellier: Université Paul Valéry, 1973.

Naslund, Sena Jeter. "Mr. Sleary's Lisp: A Note on *Hard Times.*" *Dickens Studies Newsletter* 12, no. 2 (1981): 42–46.

Nelson, Harland S. *Charles Dickens.* Boston: Twayne, 1981.

Oddie, William. "*Hard Times.*" In *Dickens and Carlyle: The Question of Influence,* 41–60. London: Centenary Press, 1972.

Orwell, George. "Charles Dickens." In *Dickens, Dali, and Others: Studies in Popular Culture.* New York: Reynal & Hitchcock, 1946.

Sadock, Geoffrey Johnston. "Dickens and Dr. Leavis: A Critical Commentary on *Hard Times.*" *Dickens Studies Annual* 2 (1972): 208–16.

Sadrin, Anny. "The Perversion of Desire: A Study of Irony as a Structural Element in *Hard Times.*" In *Studies in the Later Dickens,* edited by Jean-Claude Amalric, 93–117. Montpellier: Université Paul Valéry, 1973.

Schwarzbach, F. S. "*Hard Times:* The Industrial City." In *Dickens and the City,* 143–50. London: Athlone, 1979.

Smith, Anne. "*Hard Times* and *The Times* Newspaper." *The Dickensian* 69, no. 371 (1973): 153–62.

Spector, Stephen J. "Monsters of Metonymy: *Hard Times* and Knowing the Working Class." *ELH* 51, no. 2 (Summer 1984): 365–84.

Wilson, Angus. *The World of Charles Dickens.* New York: Viking, 1970.

Winters, Warrington. "Dickens's *Hard Times:* The Lost Childhood." *Dickens Studies Annual* 2, (1972): 217–36.

Acknowledgments

"The Industrial Novels: *Hard Times*" (originally entitled "The Industrial Novels") by Raymond Williams from *Culture and Society 1780–1950* by Raymond Williams, © 1958 by Raymond Williams. Reprinted by permission of the author, Chatto & Windus: The Hogarth Press, and Columbia University Press.

"Dickens's *Hard Times:* The Romance as Radical Literature" by Robert E. Lougy from *Dickens Studies Annual,* vol. 2, edited by Robert B. Partlow, Jr., © 1979 by AMS Press, Inc. Reprinted by permission.

"Imagery and Theme in *Hard Times*" (originally entitled *"Hard Times"*) by Robert Barnard from *Imagery and Theme in the Novels of Dickens* by Robert Barnard, © 1974 by the Norwegian Research Council for Science and the Humanities. Reprinted by permission of the author and Universitetsforlaget.

"Gradgrind and Bounderby: Character and Caricature" (originally entitled *"Hard Times"*) by Geoffrey Thurley from *The Dickens Myth: Its Genesis and Structure* by Geoffrey Thurley, © 1976 by the University of Queensland Press. Reprinted by permission.

"*Hard Times:* The News and the Novel" by Joseph Butwin from *Nineteenth Century Fiction* 32, no. 2 (September 1977), © 1977 by the Regents of the University of California. Reprinted by permission of the University of California Press.

"Muddle and Wonderful No-Meaning: Verbal Irresponsibility and Verbal Failures in *Hard Times*" by Peter Bracher from *Studies in the Novel* 10, no. 3 (Fall 1978), © 1978 by North Texas State University. Reprinted by permission.

"Polyphony and Problematic in *Hard Times*" by Roger Fowler from *The Changing World of Charles Dickens,* edited by Robert Giddings, © 1983 by Vision Press Ltd. Reprinted by permission of Vision Press Ltd., and Barnes & Noble Books, Totowa, New Jersey.

"Deconstructing *Hard Times*" (originally entitled *"Hard Times"*) by Steven Connor from *Charles Dickens* by Steven Connor, © 1985 by Steven Connor. Reprinted by permission of Basil Blackwell Publishers, Oxford.

Index

Accidents, preventable, 71-73, 74-75
Aesthetical Education of Man, An (Schiller), 33
"Amusements of the People, The," 65, 66
Anatomy of Criticism (Frye), 18
Autobiography (Mill), 57

Bachelard, Gaston, 27
Bakhtin, Mikhail, 99-101
Barnum, P. T., 66
Bentham, Jeremy, 5
Bitzer, 12, 48, 49-50
Blackpool, Stephen, 5, 11, 21, 24, 26; death of, 24-25, 49-50, 72, 79-80; on failure in communication, 77, 87, 88; on preventable accidents, 71-72; speech style of, 106-7, 108-10; vow of, to Rachael, 70-72
Bleak House, 1, 5, 23, 113-14, 119
Bounderby, Josiah, 7, 12, 26, 27; as class-emblem, 55-56; as death figure, 30; denial of childhood by, 19-20, 29; as embodiment of repressed eros, 28, 29; and fact, 116; and fictionalized image of workers, 84-85; linguistic dislocations of, 82, 89-90; and Louisa, 92-93; and mother,

29-30; and Mrs. Sparsit, 59-60; physiognomy of, 28-29, 120; speech style of, 101-2, 108-9

Caricature, 2, 9, 55-60, 100-101
Carlyle, Thomas, 4, 5, 12
Cazamian, Louis, 62
Chadwick, Edwin, 12
Characterization: by differentiation of speech, 100-112; drabness of, 5; of industrial workers, 11-12; lack of realism of, 27; metaphorical, 120-22; and will, 4-5. *See also individual characters*
Charlie (*Our Mutual Friend*), 51
Childhood, 29, 31-32, 45
Circus, 13-14, 32-33, 35-36
Civilization and Its Discontents (Freud), 23, 26, 35
Clennam, Mrs. (*Little Dorrit*), 44
Cobbett, William, 12, 13, 14
Coketown, 12, 13-15, 20-22, 27-28, 43, 69; aggression theme of, 24; and circus, 32-33, 35-36; citizens of, 21, 22-23; as death, 32; fires of, 50-52; as manifestation of psychic disorientation, 34-35; and repression of